Entrepreneurship in New York:

The Mismatch between Venture Capital and Academic R&D

Judith Albers, Ph.D.

Thomas R. Moebus

2014

ISBN: 978-0-9897226-3-6 (Print)

978-0-9897226-4-3 (Electronic)

Published by Milne Library, SUNY Geneseo, 1 College Circle, Geneseo, NY 14454

About This Report

In the summer of 2009, The State University of New York embarked on creating the first comprehensive strategic plan in the vast system's sixty-year history. Less than a year later, the University launched The Power of SUNY—an ambitious plan that grew out of dozens of intense discussions that took place across the state and included voices from all sectors. Over the course of ten months, thousands of business owners, elected officials, education experts, community leaders, students, and others came out to several town hall-style meetings and events to discuss a common, underlying concern: the state's struggling economy and what could be done—what SUNY could do—to make it flourish and create a better quality of life for all New Yorkers.

In the process of putting together The Power of SUNY, six interreliant "Big Ideas" emerged upon which the University's goals for its future—and New York's future—are built: SUNY and The Seamless Education Pipeline, SUNY and Healthier New York, SUNY and an Energy-smart New York, SUNY and the Vibrant Community, SUNY and the World, and the subject of this report, SUNY and the Entrepreneurial Century.

Research and innovation have long been mainstays of American higher education, but in the 21st century knowledge creation is no longer enough. Economic growth depends on translating knowledge into tangible, measurable benefits, from more patents used to more grants won to more jobs created. This shift demands an entrepreneurial mindset, a way of thinking that creates and shapes new markets.

The critical components that businesses of all sizes and stages need—knowledge, talent, and expertise—can all be found at SUNY. We have $1 billion annually in research expenditures, more than 10,000 research projects across the system's 64 campuses, significant infrastructure, strong existing partnerships, and some of the best faculty and students in the world. We must continually explore, aggressively, how we can combine and fine-tune our many diffuse pieces to help current and future New York companies and address national research gaps.

Because of the SUNY system's diversity—of areas of expertise, of place, of the make-up of our student body and workforce—and sheer magnitude, we are uniquely positioned to serve as New York's strongest economic driver. We take this responsibility seriously and also consider it a tremendous privilege. Marrying our core mission, To Learn, To Search, To Serve, with our profound economic development capabilities makes for a powerful combination the likes of which, we think, the nation has never before seen. We offer this report as one of many steps toward fully realizing our potential to drive entrepreneurship and innovation, and build strong, healthy communities across the Empire State.

GENESEO

Contents

Foreword

In coming to New York and SUNY in June 2012, I joined a state and university system with visionary leadership unmatched in scope, scale and diversity of talent, infrastructure and innovative thought. Together New York and SUNY are charting new paths to economic development and entrepreneurial opportunity.

The timing of this study by the SUNY Levin Institute is opportune. Governor Cuomo has set forth a comprehensive Innovation Agenda that includes START-UP NY, Innovation "Hot Spots," the New York State Venture Capital Fund and the Innovation New York Network. These programs and platforms work together to foster entrepreneurialism and economic growth through public-private partnerships that give researchers the tools they need to bring their ideas to market.

START-UP New York will transform SUNY campuses and other university communities across the state into tax-free communities for new and expanding businesses. Innovation Hot Spots in all regions will help innovators and entrepreneurs grow new companies, invest new funds to support start-up enterprises, and establish an Innovation New York Network that connects entrepreneurs with investors, customers, and talent from around the State and beyond to "turbocharge" New York's innovation economy.

SUNY's Chancellor, Nancy Zimpher, has shaped SUNY's leading role to revitalize New York's economy, bringing forward the power of its sixty-five campuses—each within an hour's drive of every citizen of the State. Indeed the Power of SUNY is a primary engine driving New York's economy.

With that and other key partnerships in place, New York has unlimited and untapped potential. New York's ranking as #2 in the nation in R&D expenditures at its universities is a testament to the excellence and energy of its academics in both the public and private sector. Its lower ranking of entrepreneurial outcomes from this R&D compared to other states such as California and Massachusetts is what gives us the chance to improve.

Thanks to our colleagues at the SUNY Levin Institute, *the Entrepreneurship in New York Study* gives precise focus to this opportunity and instructs us on how best to raise our game and our standing. It provides essential data and identifies the unique features of New York's innovation and investment climate on which we need to confidently and actively rely.

Dr. Tim Killeen
President, The Research Foundation for SUNY
SUNY Vice Chancellor for Research

Acknowledgments

SUNY Geneseo is pleased to be supporting the publication of this research essay on entrepreneurship in New York. The project was initiated by the Levin Institute and the SUNY Research Foundation and has been brought to completion through the collaboration of the State University of New York system administration and SUNY Geneseo. As key players in the New York State entrepreneurial ecosystem, the co-authors of this work, Dr. Judith Albers and Thomas R. Moebus, have brought to us a careful analysis of the relationship between venture capital and academic research and development in the state of New York. This paper is relevant for both upstate and downstate entrepreneurs as well as stakeholders in the entrepreneurial community state-wide. On the basis of their data, they suggest a number of strategies and tactics for improving the alignment of capital and research and for energizing innovation and enterprise throughout the state.

Geneseo is particularly proud to be the academic home of Dr. Judith Albers, who recently became the inaugural holder of the Charles L. "Bud" VanArsdale Chair in Entrepreneurship. Housed in the Geneseo School of Business, this Chair is supported by a gift from Bud VanArsdale, former President of the Bank of Castile and long-time benefactor of SUNY Geneseo. Dr. Albers is dedicated to providing entrepreneurial learning across the curriculum. By joining forces with Tom Moebus, the Director of Investor Development for SUNY Research Foundation, she is able to "bring theory to practice." Together, and along with many colleagues across SUNY, they are helping to fulfill SUNY's promise to advance the Entrepreneurial Century.

The publication of this work is possible not only because of the support of the SUNY system, but also because of the innovative scholarly publishing efforts of Geneseo's Milne Library and its staff. Special thanks for their support to Library Director Cyril Oberlander, Dr. Daniel Julius of the Levin Institute, Dr. Tim Killeen, President of the Research Foundation, and Chancellor Nancy Zimpher.

Dr. Carol S. Long
Interim President
SUNY Geneseo

I. Introduction to The Entrepreneurship in New York Project

This is an auspicious time for innovation and entrepreneurship in the State of New York. In his 2013 State of the State speech, Governor Andrew M. Cuomo addressed what continues to be a significant economic conundrum, i.e., the transfer of innovative technologies from academia to start-up companies. *"We're doing the research, we've developed the ideas, we have the academic institutions: we're not making the transference to commercialization."* The governor established an ambitious statewide innovation agenda to improve New York's performance in creating new businesses and deriving economic benefit from its vast research and development assets. Building on the established Regional Economic Development Councils, the governor proposed:

- The formation of ten regional Innovation Hot-Spots;

- A $50 million public fund for innovation-based early stage companies;

- Landmark START-UP NY legislation, aimed at growing new businesses in tax-free enclaves on SUNY campuses, as well as other academic institutions in the state; and

- Integrating these activities through an Innovation New York Network.

The *Entrepreneurship in New York Project* (ENY) builds on *New York in the World*, a 2011 SUNY Levin Institute study on the impact of globalization on New York City and State. This earlier study, conducted with the Center for an Urban Future, catalogued the economic evolution of both downstate and upstate New York in the era of globalization and provided an understanding of how and where New York State has prospered, and where it has not—a challenging presentation of the upstate-downstate divide. The "Road Ahead" section recommended a growth strategy for the New Global Economy, built on five important dimensions:

- Promote and support entrepreneurship;

- Build upon the state's R&D assets to expand the Innovation Economy;

- Help more New York businesses export and compete globally;

- View colleges and universities as economic drivers for regional growth; and

- Improve connections between upstate cities and New York City.

In light of the findings of *New York in the World*, and the importance of a new state innovation agenda, the goals of the *Entrepreneurship in New York Project* are to:

- **Better understand the realities** of innovation and entrepreneurship in New York's cities and regions, as linked to university-based R&D and investing patterns;

- **Establish a baseline of current entrepreneurial success and potential** using metrics such as number of companies, regional and sector performance, and economic impacts; and

- **Detail the formation of innovation-based companies** and measure the success of current and future initiatives to stimulate the translation of innovation into commerce.

Entrepreneurship in New York plans to meet these goals through a series of reports delivered in sequence. This first report compares and contrasts university-based R&D and private investment in innovation. The next report will provide an accurate assessment of university-related entrepreneurship in the state. It is intended to serve as a baseline against which progress of New York's innovation agenda can be measured. Follow-up reports will help to understand best practices and novel initiatives for establishing start-ups and supporting their success.

II. Executive Summary

This first ENY report is focused on understanding venture capital (VC) and academic R&D, which have historically been two critical assets in the development of any entrepreneurial ecosystem, and which relate to important concerns expressed by Governor Cuomo in January 2013. In his State of the State speech, the governor cited several "Troubling Tech Transfer Facts" from earlier published papers based on 2007 data.[1]

New York universities rank second nationally in total research spending with nearly $4B spent annually; California ranks first with $6.5B.[2] However,

- New York attracts only 4% of the nation's VC investment while California attracts 47%;

- New York's colleges incubate fewer new companies, with 35 start-ups launched in 2007, while California schools had 58 and Massachusetts's schools had 60; and

- New York is home to fewer fast-growing technology companies, with only 11 on the Deloitte Technology Fast 500 List, as compared with California's 169 and Massachusetts's 46.

Since 2007, there has been a significant enhancement in the entrepreneurial ecosystem and investment climate in New York City. But for most of New York State, the situation is not much improved and the message is unfortunately still unchanged in 2013. NYS continues to **lead** nationally for academic research but **lag** nationally for entrepreneurial performance and investment dollars relative to California and Massachusetts. Speaking on this disparity between research and commercialization, Cuomo stated, *"That gap is what we have to fix."*

In this report we present and examine financial data relevant to understanding the patterns of innovation, investment, and entrepreneurship in New York:

Section III: Venture Capital Investing Patterns. California leads all states by far, including New York, in the management of venture capital and in received venture investments. In recent years, New York has garnered progressively more investments but has been challenged to close in on the order of magnitude lead that California has had and continues to enjoy.

Section IV: What Interests Investors. Venture investors have historically invested broadly, but increasingly now focus on Internet opportunities. That interest has intensified in recent years, and is especially pronounced in New York where recent investing has been almost exclusively focused on Internet, mobile, and other digital businesses. This is in stark contrast to comparative states of California and Massachusetts, which demonstrate more balanced investments across many different sectors and fields.

---

[1] "Venture Capital and Seed Activity in New York State", by Excell Partners, Feb and May 2009, and "Governor's Task Force on Diversifying the New York State Economy through Industry-Higher Education Partnership", Dec 2009.

[2] National Science Foundation (NSF) Higher Education Research and Development (HERD) Report, 2007.

Section V: Venture Investing in New York. Venture investing in New York State is bifurcated dramatically along geographic lines. While New York City is basking in a significant uptick in start-up capital, venture investing in upstate New York is almost non-existent. This has severe consequences on the formation of a robust ecosystem for building new businesses.

Section VI: Academic R&D Expenditures. New York is a strong and consistent #2 nationally behind California in university-based R&D expenditures. Academic assets are balanced across the state. Nearly every region in New York has an opportunity to leverage its university-based assets to create start-ups, that is, if capital and talent are available to launch new companies. Academic researchers, however, are focused on the hard sciences, i.e., industries that appear to be losing favor with VCs, particularly in New York State.

Section VII: Mismatched Interests. When the data for venture investing in New York are juxtaposed with the data for university-based R&D, one observes a significant misalignment between the interests of investors (in digital technologies) and of the academic research community (in the hard sciences). This could be a significant obstacle to the commercialization of university technologies and the creation of innovation-based spin-outs in New York. We are unaware of any other report that has acknowledged this situation. The data will show how dramatic this misalignment is in New York, as compared to California and Massachusetts, and especially as it relates to the life sciences.

This unique profile of academic research and private investment in New York presents a challenge, offers an opportunity, and prompts some thoughts for consideration.

A Challenge: The governor has posed a challenge and initiatives to improve technology transfer and accelerate the commercialization of university-based innovation. Acceleration will be difficult without a near, knowledgeable, and engaged cadre of investors who are interested in the hard sciences and willing to help create and grow businesses built on Life and Physical Science research. In New York State, the wider difference in interest between investors and academic researchers, compared with California and Massachusetts, poses a significant challenge. Fixing the mismatched interests between investors and researchers may require creative actions, for instance, engaging the investor communities in California and Massachusetts.

An Opportunity: New York City VCs and angels are capitalizing on the city's emerging strengths in "soft tech." This trend is beneficial for the NYC economy, entrepreneurial community, and investor returns. The success of the "NYC paradigm" in growing entrepreneurial businesses over the past five years, *without great contribution from university R&D*, should be explored for its potential economic benefit. START-UP NY may offer the chance for many kinds of university-business alliances to form upstate, based on creative and commercial services and IT applications. Opportunities to design mutually beneficial partnerships to grow innovative businesses upstate based on this model should be considered.

For Consideration: The alignment and adequacy of capital and R&D, in both type and quantity, is essential to the success of an innovation economy. These investment streams operate best when matched and balanced regionally, and in New York's case, across regions. This balance is currently not observed in New York and the situation must be understood and addressed in order to develop an enduring and successful innovation agenda that serves all parts of the state.

Note: Unless otherwise indicated, all venture capital data in this report is derived from the National Venture Capital Association (NVCA) Annual Reports 2008-2013 and www.pwcmoneytree.com. All data pertaining to academic R&D is derived from the National Science Foundation (NSF) Higher Education Research and Development (HERD) Reports from 2008-2011. A detail methodology section is provided in Appendix B.

III. Venture Capital Investing Patterns

There is wide agreement among policy makers on the importance of entrepreneurial companies to economic growth and well-being. Venture capital (VC) is a major driver of that entrepreneurial economy. The nation continues to look to this sector for job creation, economic development, better healthcare, cleaner technology, and a faster, better, and more secure internet. (National Venture Capital Association Yearbook 2013)

In today's economy, there is wide agreement by policy makers on the importance of entrepreneurial companies, but often times it seems that policy makers do not understand how entrepreneurship happens, especially for innovation-based companies. Significant capital is required, in stages, to launch these companies and successfully position their high-tech products in the market. Generally the more sophisticated the technical basis of a company, the more venture capital is required. Because of the high sophistication level of university-based research in the hard sciences, venture capital is vitally important to its translation into commercial ventures.

It behooves stakeholders to understand how much venture capital is available and being invested in New York State and what industries the VCs are focused on. To provide context at the state level, this study starts by looking at VC investing at the national level.

National VC Investments. Figure 2.1 below shows national VC investments for the last five years.

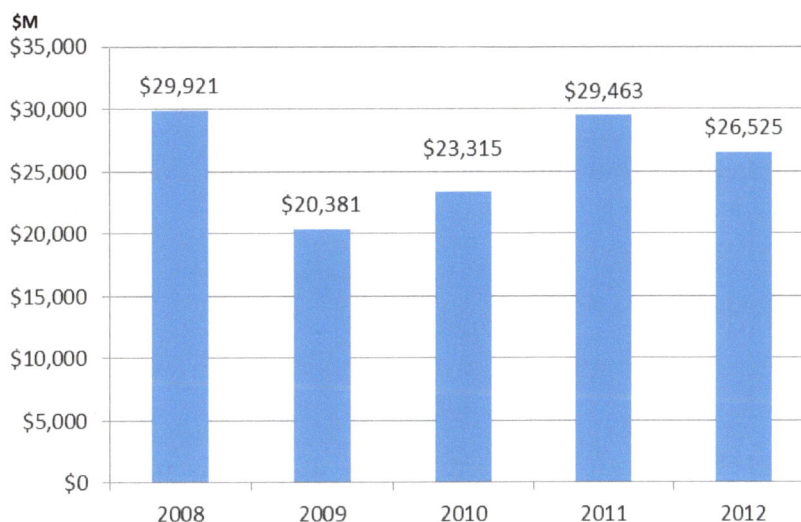

Figure 2.1: National Venture Capital Investment, 2008-2012

As evidenced in 2009, there was a bit of a dip in venture capital after the market crash, but investing has recovered, and in general has held fairly steady nationally in the $20-30 billion range. Note however, that unlike academic R&D funding, which will be discussed in a later section of this report, and where the government consistently increases spending year after year, VC funding is subject to market variability.

A bit unusual is the fact that venture capital is highly concentrated in very few states, primarily California, Massachusetts, and New York. In an attempt to profile these states,

7

Figure 2.2 again shows overall U.S. investing for the last five years in blue juxtaposed with bars that represent percent of total for these states of interest.

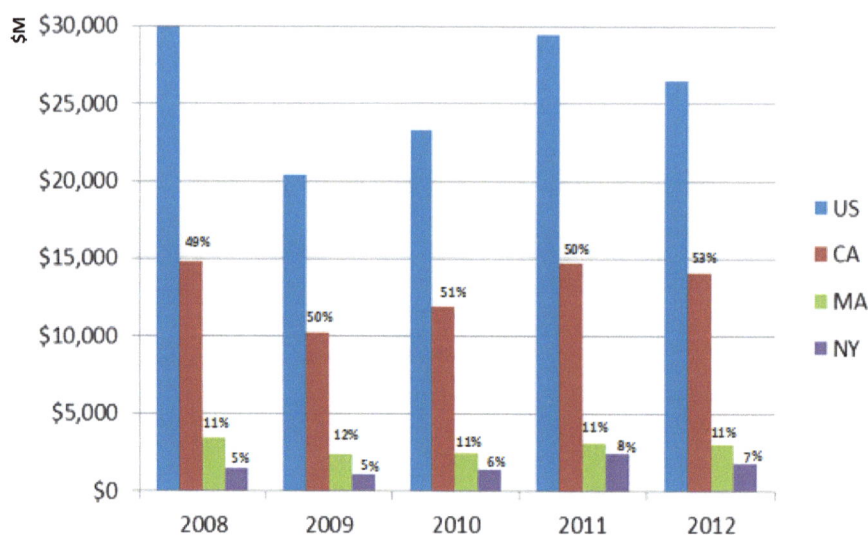

Figure 2.2: Top Three States for VC Investments, 2008-2012

It is obvious from this figure that California dominates the industry. Every year, regardless of the specific amount invested, or whether the market waxes or wanes, California receives at or over 50% of the nation's venture capital, and as the bars indicate, the trend has been upwards in the last five years. Every year, more and more capital ends up (percentage-wise) in California.

Massachusetts ranks second in the nation for VC investments, holding steady at about 11%. New York ranks third but at a fraction of California's total. In the last five years, New York has trended slightly upwards. This allows us to update one of the governor's Troubling Tech Transfer Facts:

- **In 2007**, New York attracted only 4% of the nation's VC investments while California attracted 47%.

- **In 2012**, New York attracted 7% of the nation's VC investments while California attracted 53%.

While many New Yorkers are taking great pride in the 2012 uptick, New York is still hugely behind California as it relates to venture capital.

Not shown on this graph are the other top states. Texas and Washington almost always rank either as fourth or fifth in the nation but with a very small percent of 2-3% of the national total each. All other 45 states share the remainder, meaning that they each receive 0-1% of whatever is left.

Investments vs. Deals. Figure 2.3 summarizes and averages out the VC investments for the top three states over the last five years. California received about $13B each year for an average of 51% of the national total, compared to New York, which received about $1.7B each year for an average of 6% of the national total.

State	Average Investment($M) 2008-2012	Avg % of Total
CA	$13,163	51%
MA	$2,891	11%
NY	$1,654	6%
US Total	$25,954	100%

Figure 2.3: VC Investments for Top Three States

Relative to numbers of transactions, or deals, as shown in Figure 2.4, California saw about 1,500 VC deals each year for an average of 41% of the total, compared to New York, which saw nearly 300 deals each year for an average of 8% of the total.

State	Average Number of Deals 2008-2012	Avg % of Total
CA	1,513	41%
MA	396	11%
NY	288	8%
US Total	3,720	100%

Figure 2.4: VC Deals for Top Three States

If, per state, average investments in Table 2.3 are divided by average number of deals in Table 2.4, the resulting quotient is average deal size. Figure 2.5 shows that the average deal size in the U.S. is $6.9M. Average deal size is significantly higher in California at $8.7M per deal, Massachusetts is at $7.3M per deal, and NY is below the national average at $5.7M per deal.

State	Average Deal Size ($M) 2008-2012
CA	$8.7
MA	$7.3
NY	$5.7
US Avg	$6.9

Figure 2.5: VC Deal Size for Top Three States

Deal size quantities could be related to the *types* of deals that are being made in these regions. As will be seen in the next section, most of the New York deals are in digital technologies (IT, software, media) and those deals are generally not as capital intensive as many of the Life and Physical Science deals that are being transacted in California and Massachusetts.

Capital under Management. The data already presented refers to venture capital that is being **received** by a state or region on an annual basis. This is not the same as capital **under management**, i.e., how much money VCs have available to deploy.

State	Average Amount ($M) 2008-2012	Avg % of Total
CA	$91,605	47%
MA	$33,860	17%
NY	$17,827	9%
US Total	$195,280	100%

Figure 2.6: Capital under Management, 2008-2012

As shown in Figure 2.6 above, California, Massachusetts, and New York are again the top three states for capital under management. As a side note, the financial collapse on Wall Street in 2008 caused a 30% drop in capital under management in the U.S. California and Massachusetts were somewhat affected but the worst hit was New York, where investors saw a 50% drop. Between 2003 and 2007, New York investors averaged $33B under management. By 2008-2012, it was down to $18B. This drop could mean that, moving forward, VCs will be trying to get higher returns with less money and possibly keeping their monies closer to home. That possibility actually suggests a good question: Do VCs typically invest close to home?

In-State Investing. The first column of Figure 2.7 shows average capital deployed annually by-state. The second column shows average capital that remained in-state. And the final column shows the average percent that remained in-state.

State	Average Capital Deployed Annually by State ($M) 2008-2012	Avg Capital that Remained In-State Annually ($M) 2008-2012	Avg % that Remained In-State 2008-2012
CA	$8,569	$6,103	71%
MA	$2,569	$871	34%
NY	$2,080	$351	17%

Figure 2.7: In-State Investing, 2008-2012

California VCs kept 71% in-state, investing only 6% in Massachusetts, 4% in New York, and 19% in the rest of the world. It appears that California VCs primarily support California entrepreneurs or entrepreneurs who move to California.

Massachusetts VCs invested 34% in-state, investing a matching 34% in California, 8% in New York, and dispersing 24% to the rest of the world.

New York VCs only invested 17% in-state and sent 83% out of state. While that is not great news for start-up companies in New York State, it is better than previously reported. In papers based on 2007 data,[3] it was noted that New York VCs were only investing 9% in-state and 91% out-of-state. These current numbers represent a significant improvement—but not for upstate. As later data will show, "in-state" investing really means in or around New York City, while upstate New York continues to starve for investment capital.

Of the 83% sent out of state, New York VCs continue to be very generous to California: 39% of New York monies leave the east coast for the west coast because that is possibly

[3] "Venture Capital and Seed Activity in New York State," by Excell Partners, Feb and May 2009.

where the best deals are. Massachusetts receives 10%, and 34% of the monies go to other states and countries.

Investing by Stage, Nationally. It is also important to look at investments by stage of development, especially since there has been a notable change in investing trends/patterns over the last decade. Going back a decade in time, the statistics show that VCs clearly had a preference for investing "later." Just under 40% of all investing was in later stage companies; just under 40% in expansion stage companies; just under 20% in early stage companies; and only about 4% in seed stage. This pattern was still true in 2008.

However, the bars in Figure 2.8 show a notable increase in early stage investing to the point where it's nearly an equal third with expansion and later stage.

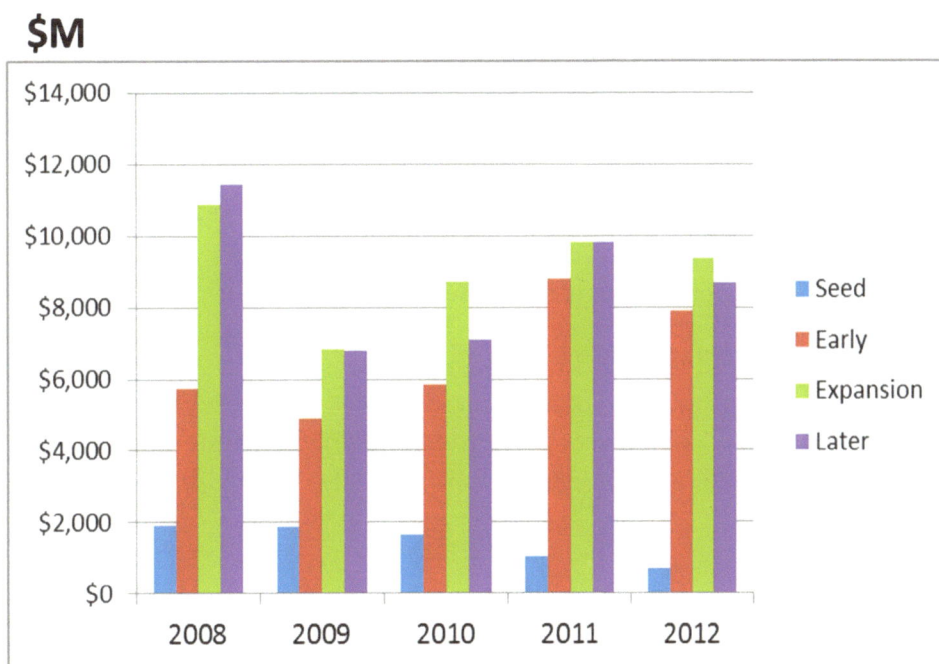

Figure 2.8: National Investments by Development Stage, 2008-2012

Seed stage investing remains at about 3% of the total, trending downward. The data indicate that seed investing is of lesser interest to VCs. Lack of seed funding for start-up companies has historically been and continues to be a major problem nationally, especially for hard science companies requiring considerable sums to successfully pass through the "Valley of Death."[4]

Section Summary. The data in this section can be summarized as follows. While venture capital is subject to market variability, it has remained between $20-30B for the last five year. It is highly concentrated in three states—California, Massachusetts, and New York—with California dominating the other states by an order of magnitude. Not only does California lead (by far) in the amount of venture capital it receives annually, but its percent of the national total increases every year. It also dominates (by far) in the amount of venture capital under management. Further, California VCs invest close to home: a remarkable 71% of the capital deployed by California VCs remains in-state. Possibly Californians VCs believe/recognize that the entrepreneurial culture that best favors a high ROI is in their

---

[4] "Venture Capital and Seed Activity in New York State," by Excell Partners, Feb and May 2009.

own backyard. Also, the deal size in California is larger than the average deal size in the U.S., including in Massachusetts and New York.

Massachusetts is consistently between California and New York, but actually its numbers are closer to New York's than California's. New York is consistently coming in third based on the criteria used here. Although showing some recent signs of improvement, New York is still seriously trailing California.

The only good news for start-up companies is that VCs have started investing more at the early stage again (but still not seed), as opposed to previous years where the focus was heavily on expansion and later stage investing.

The reader should now have a good foundational understanding of venture capitalists, where they are, how much money they have, and how much they deploy. But there has been no information provided yet regarding their investing preferences relative to industry. Are they interested in Life and Physical Sciences, i.e., the hard sciences? Or are they interested in Information Technology and Creative & Commerce, i.e., digital technologies?

Loosely defining venture investments as high-tech has done a disservice to an accurate understanding of what VCs really invest in. A dissection of the phrase "high-tech" is proposed in Figure 2.9. High-tech can be divided into two very broad categories of the Hard Sciences and Digital Technologies. The Hard Sciences can be further subdivided into **Life Sciences** and **Physical Sciences**. Digital Technologies can be further subdivided into **Information Technologies** and what will here be called **Creative & Commerce**. This latter category combines many application and service sectors such as media, entertainment, finance, education, retail, etc. These four categories include the 16 specific industries defined by the National Venture Capital Association (NVCA) as shown in the gray boxes in Figure 2.9.

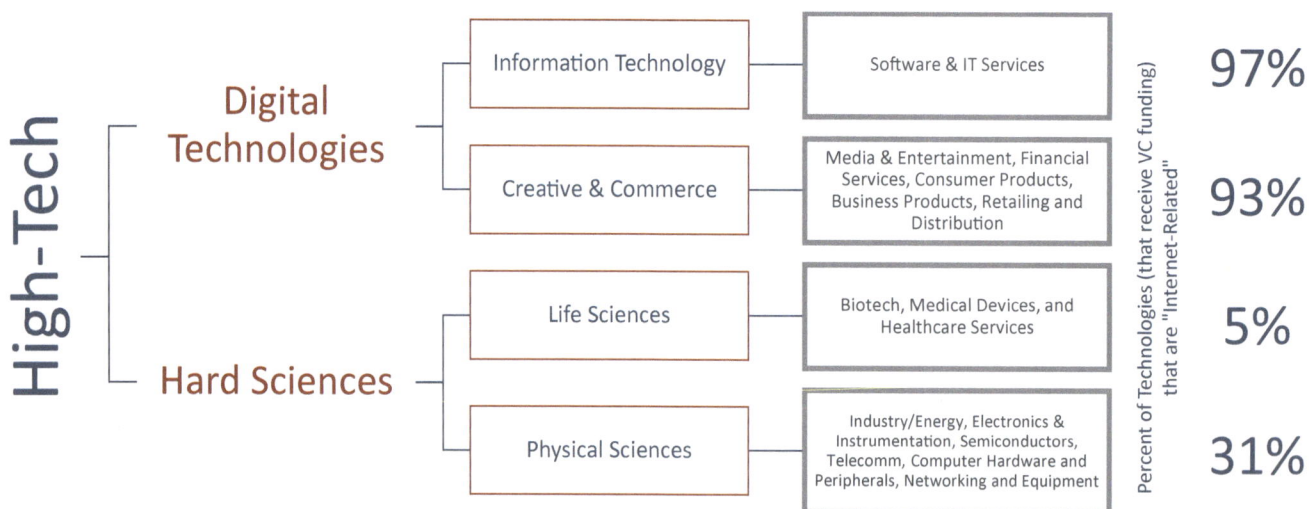

Figure 2.9: Defining and Grouping Industries

It will also be important shortly to consider how much VC activity is Internet related. But the Internet is really not a single industry; rather, it is a classification that spans the spectrum of industries. Therefore each industry category has been tagged with a value that indicates the percent of investable businesses in that category that are "Internet related." For example, 97% of all investable IT companies are offering technologies and services that are Internet-related.

Armed with this terminology and categorization, the authors and readers are equipped for the next section to explore the kinds of high-tech opportunities that VCs are pursuing most aggressively.

IV. What Interests Investors

Historical View. This section starts with a big picture, historical view of VC investing, because it is important to note that VCs have long had a fascination or a particular interest in the Internet.

Figure 3.1 extends all the way back to 1985, before there was an Internet. Note that prior to 1985, VC activity was modest and the translation of academic research was barely a thought in anyone's mind. But in 1980, the U.S. Congress passed the Bayh-Dole Act, which allowed for the commercialization of federally funded research. It was in the years following that universities slowly started establishing tech-transfer offices, and VCs started taking an interest in the very sophisticated technologies that were coming out of the universities. Of course, the genesis of all this was in Boston and Silicon Valley. The life sciences (biotech) and physical sciences (semiconductors) were areas of significant interest to the VCs at least from 1985 to 1995. But then came the Internet.

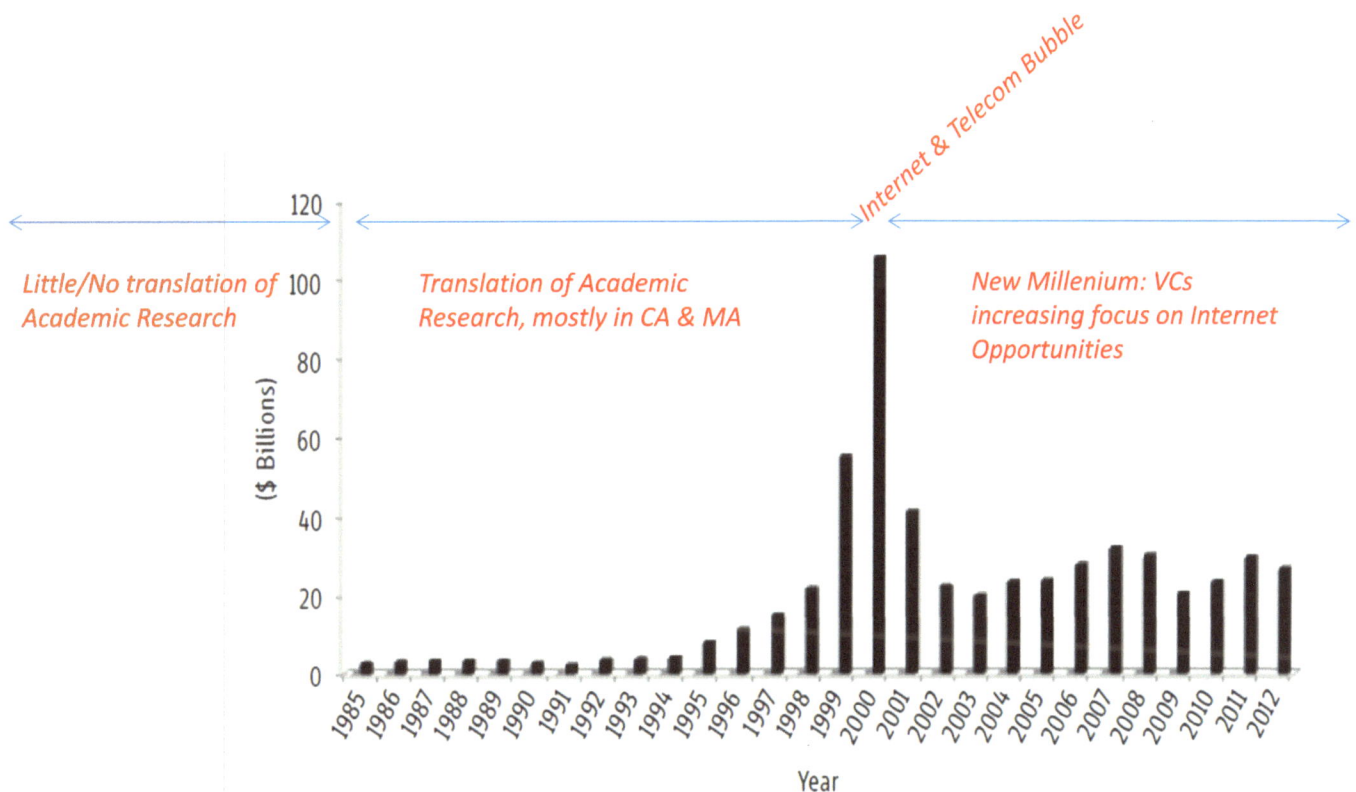

Figure 3.1: 30 Year Trends in VC Investing

Internet-Related Investments. Figure 3.2 shows Internet-related investments from 1995 to 2012, and the profile should look familiar. VCs started investing in the Internet around 1995, and their fascination with Internet opportunities has literally shaped the profile of their investing patterns. In fact, the excitement over the Internet caused an overly zealous investing spree resulting in the dot-com and telecommunications bubble in the year 2000. Over $100B was invested, and 80% of that was in Internet-related opportunities.

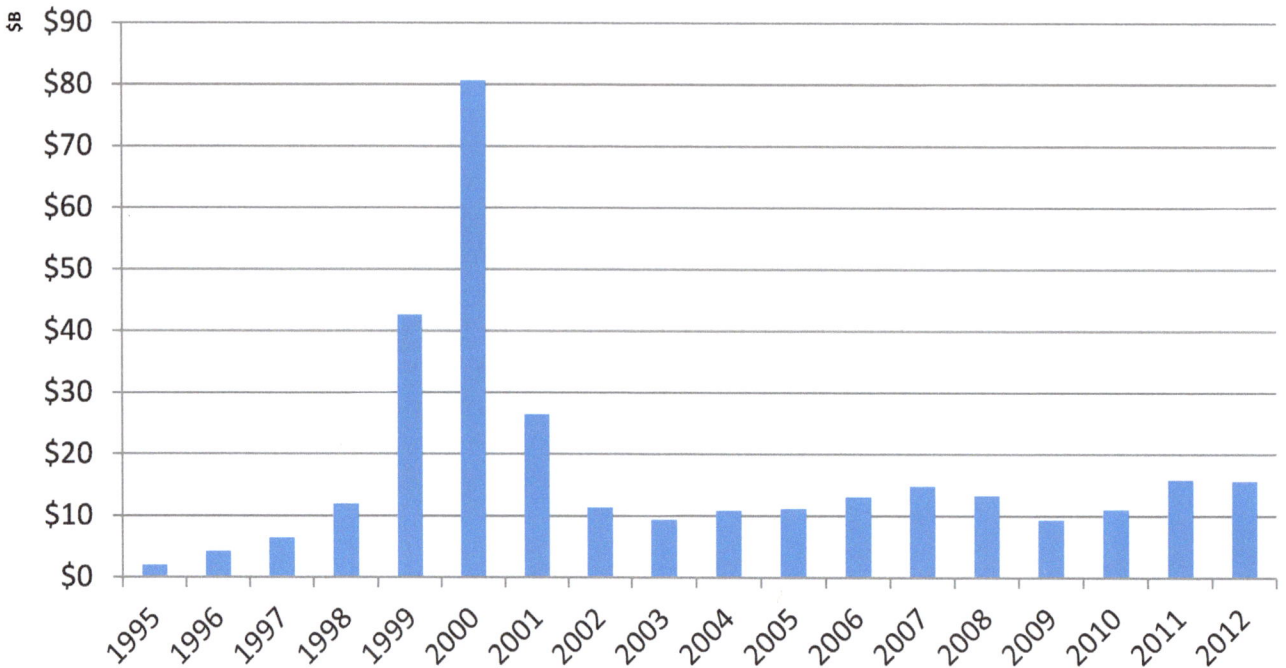

Figure 3.2: 20 Year Trends in Internet Investing

Certainly after the bubble burst, things calmed down a bit, but since then, software and IT services have continued as the largest industry sectors for VC investing.

Investing by Industry. With that historical perspective, the study is refocused back to the last five years and recent investing trends, this time exploring the four primary industry sectors defined in the previous section:

Digital Technologies {
- Information Technology
- Creative & Commerce (Media, Entertainment, Financial Services, etc.)

Hard Sciences {
- Life Sciences
- Physical Sciences

Investing in Information Technology and Creative & Commerce over the last five years is shown in Figure 3.3, while Life and Physical Science investing is shown in Figure 3.4.

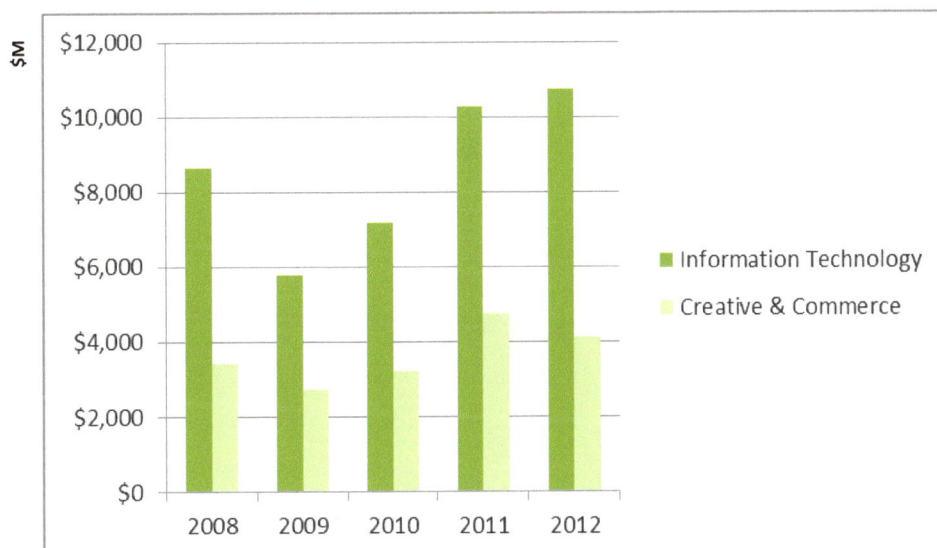

Figure 3.3: VC Investments in IT and Creative & Commerce, Nationally, 2008-2012

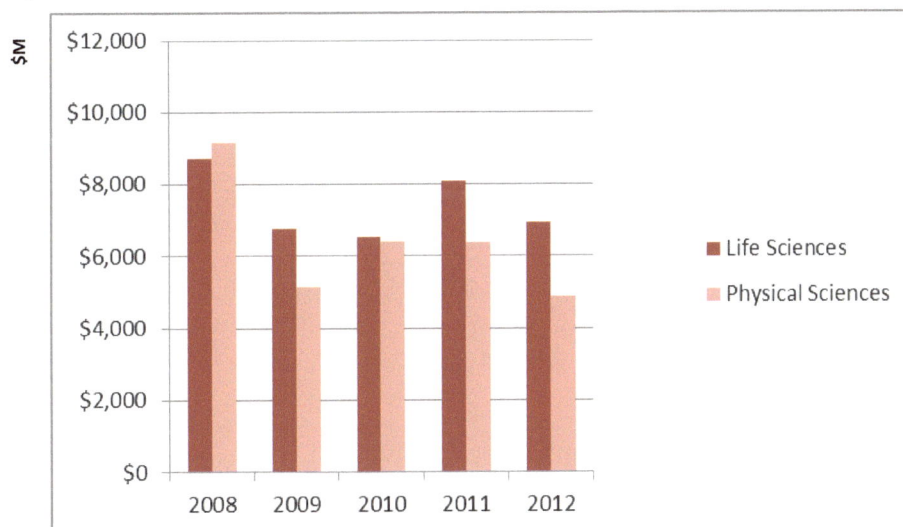

Figure 3.4: VC Investments in Life and Physical Sciences, Nationally, 2008-2012

There seems to be a pattern: Investing in IT and Creative & Commerce has been increasing in recent years, and investing in the Life and Physical Sciences has been decreasing. Specific numbers for most recent investing in 2012 show that 40% of all investments went to IT, another 16% to Creative & Commerce, 26% to Life Sciences, and 18% to Physical Sciences.

While not shown here, a look at the number of deals brokered in these industries would indicate an even more obvious pattern of "digital domination." In 2012, 44% of all deals were IT, another 16% were Creative & Commerce, 22% were Life Sciences, and 18% were Physical Sciences.

Clean Tech Trends. Given the decreasing interest in the physical sciences, some might wonder about clean tech or energy opportunities. It certainly seems as though there's been a lot of interest and support for energy lately. Are there any interesting patterns to note?

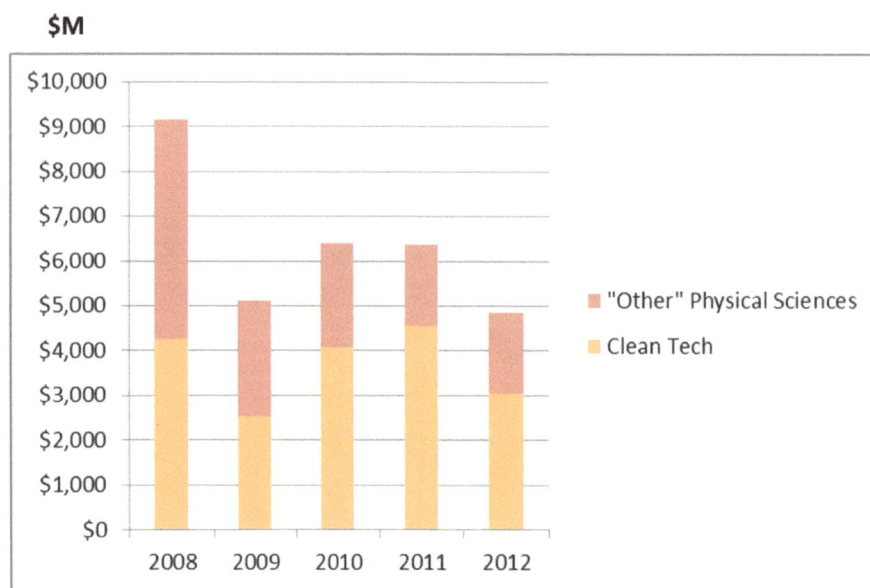

Figure 3.5: Clean Tech Investing, 2008-2012

As shown in Figure 3.5, clean tech is a **subset** of the physical sciences. It appears that clean tech has played a major role in attracting capital to this industry. In 2008-2009, clean tech received about half of all investments in the physical sciences. In 2010-2011, clean tech's percentage of total physical science investing appeared to increase, but overall there was a significant drop off in interest in the physical sciences in 2012.

The bottom line is that clean tech or energy investing is still not nearly as interesting as IT and all the excitement about clean tech does not seem to be manifesting itself heavily in VC investing.

More on IT/Internet. Not to belabor the impact of the Internet on VC, but to thoroughly understand it, the following should be noted. While the assumption can be made that the vast majority of IT/software investments are Internet related, the fact remains that majority might not mean 100%. On the flip side, it can be assumed that the vast majority of Life Science deals are not Internet related. However there might indeed be some opportunities (like Health IT) that are Internet-related.

So the 2012 NVCA statistics were reviewed for all investments across all industries and it was determined (as reported previously in Figure 2.9) that Internet-related opportunities constituted:

- 97% of all investments in Information Technology;

- 93% of all investments in Creative & Commerce;

- Possibly somewhat surprising, 31% of all Physical Science investments; and

- Only 5% of all Life Science investments.

In total, 59% of all *investments* across all industries were Internet related, and 65% of all *deals* across all industries were Internet related. That only leaves a minority percent of all investments and deals that are truly hard science deals that are not Internet related. With regard to initial investments to launch companies, the weighting was even more imbalanced, with 73% of all dollars (and 74% of all deals) going to support Internet-related companies.

Obvious Reasons. After looking at several figures in succession, which obviously indicate that VCs have a strong and growing bias toward investing in Internet-related companies, the question provoked is *Why?* That question has some obvious answers.

Internet-related companies tend to be much easier to grow and manage. They are quicker to market, lower cost, and lower risk. Often the business ideas are coming from a young demographic—there are vast numbers of students in their dorm rooms writing software and developing new apps and social networking websites. There is an entire generation of students all striving to be the next Mark Zuckerberg. This younger generation has the time for Y-combinator, Tech Stars, Start-up Weekend—programs customized for IT and the Internet. If VCs have expertise in SW/IT/Internet not the hard sciences, then this is where they'll invest. (The same can be said of angel investors.)

Hard science companies are harder and riskier. Life Science companies in particular are very difficult. It can take many years to develop and take a new drug to market. It is very costly, high risk, and there are many regulatory hurdles. Technologies are being developed by high-level university professors, who are preoccupied with their "day jobs." They have a full teaching load. They are writing grant proposals and monitoring graduate students and post-docs in their labs. Pitching business ideas can be difficult for these scientists, and due diligence can be complicated for the VCs, who may not have life science expertise. Many VCs purposely avoid life sciences because of these myriad challenges.

IPOs and Acquisitions. Regardless of what is easy versus what is difficult, VCs will "follow the money" because that is their job. VCs must exit their deals and maximize returns on their investment. The data for Initial Public Offerings (IPOs) and Acquisitions were examined to determine which companies are giving VCs their best exits.

In 2012, IPO data show that:

- 4 Media and Entertainment companies brought in a whopping $16.2B;

- 15 Software and IT service companies brought in $2.7B;

- 13 Biotech and Medical Device companies brought in just under $1B; and

- 3 Industrial and Energy companies brought in about $250M.

In 2012, Acquisition data show that:

- 202 Software and IT Services companies were sold for a total of $7.2B;

- 59 Biotech and Medical Device companies were acquired for $4.4B;

- 43 Media and Entertainment companies were acquired for $2.3B; and

- 31 Industrial and Energy companies brought in $1.1B.

These results are summarized in Figure 3.6, which shows that the easier opportunities in IT and Creative & Commerce are bringing in four times as much in returns as the harder opportunities in the Life and Physical Sciences. It is no surprise that the VC industry is trending as it is, and it is possibly unlikely that this trend will change anytime soon.

Industry Group	Information Technology	Creative & Commerce	Life Sciences	Physical Sciences
IPO	$2.7 B	$16.2 B	$1.0 B	$0.3 B
Aquisition	$7.2 B	$2.3 B	$4.4 B	$1.1 B
Total	$28.4 B		$6.7 B	

Figure 3.6: IPOs & Acquisitions, Total Returns by Industry

Section Summary. In this section, the data has shown that the Internet plays a dominant role in VC investing, and that dominance also extends to the other Creative & Commerce industries, especially Media and Entertainment companies.

What is of significance is that upon a more thorough analysis, 2012 data indicate:

- 59% of all investments were Internet related; and

- 73% of all *initial* investments were Internet related.

These statistics are depressing for Life and Physical Science start-up companies that have no application to the Internet.

As will be observed in a following section (and albeit with many goals other than economic development), the U.S. government continues to pour billions of dollars into hard science research in all fifty states. Yet, a hard science company with no application to the Internet and which is not based in California or Massachusetts has a slim chance of getting any kind of VC investment to move forward.

Even though a Section Summary has already been provided, there is still one question that remains unasked about Internet investment. Where is Internet investing occurring?

Internet Investment by State. Again, the top three states, California, Massachusetts, and New York, are shown in Figure 3.7. What is interesting here is that, in this one category, *New York has surpassed Massachusetts*. Indeed, a major report was published recently indicating that New York City has become a digital media mecca and has surpassed Boston in that realm.[5] Of course, California still dominates by a long shot.

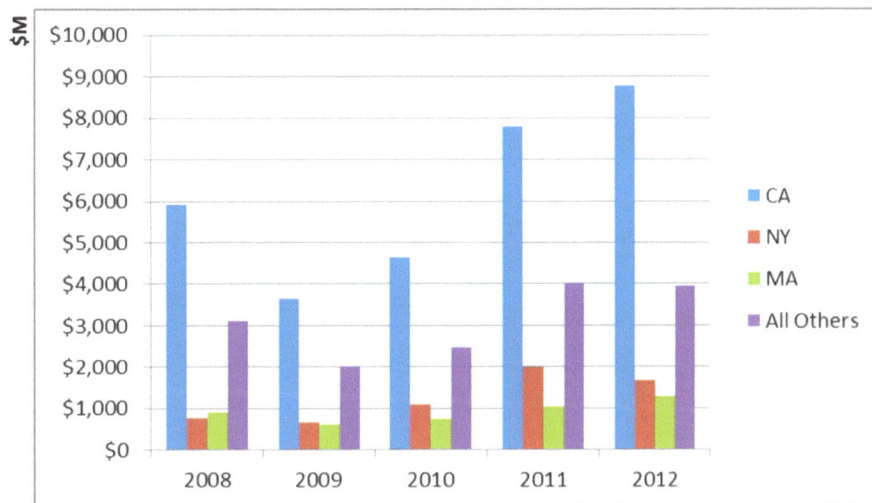

Figure 3.7: Internet Investing by State, 2008-2012

In this discussion of Internet investing in New York, a question could arise as to upstate's participation in this activity. Had this question been addressed by adding bars to the graph shown in Figure 3.7 for upstate, they would have essentially been invisible. The lack of upstate's participation means that when investing in New York is being discussed for Internet deals, it is clear that "New York" really means New York City. Upstate New York is hardly a blip on the radar for these investments.

So, an additional statement can be added to the Section Summary, which is that NY, which has been trailing behind California and Massachusetts in every category up until now, now surpasses Massachusetts for Internet investing (although California still dominates). The Internet and other digital technologies dominate in NYC.

---

[5] "New Tech City," Center for an Urban Future, May 2012.

V. Venture Capital in New York

While looking at the national context of VC investing patterns and favored industries is interesting and important, this project is fundamentally about New York State and that focus must be maintained in compiling information that might be helpful to the successful expansion of New York's innovation economy. Therefore, in this next section, the focus centers just on New York.

Funding for New York State. It was previously determined that for the last five years, New York State has received on average 6% of the national total, even though it ranks as the third highest state for venture capital. Figure 4.1 shows the actual amounts broken out from 2008-2012. VC funding is market sensitive, and in New York State, it has ranged from $1.1B to $2.5B over the last five years, averaging $1.7B per year.

While the data are compiled for the state, it is important to look more granularly to recognize, that as shown in Figure 4.1, almost all of this VC funding is going to New York City.[6]

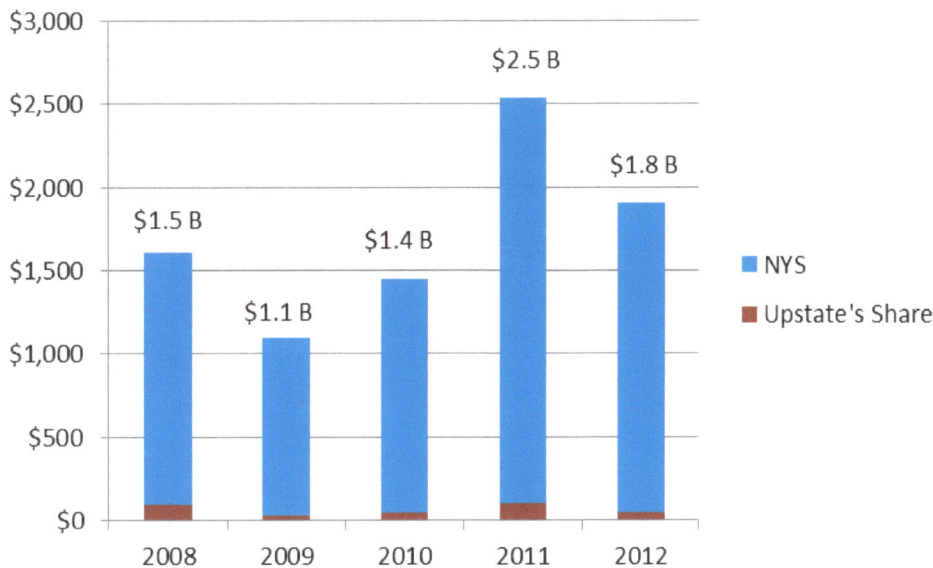

Figure 4.1: VC Investments, NYS, 2008-2012

Every year, upstate New York receives about 3-4% of the state's total investment, essentially a negligible amount. While investments downstate are increasing, upstate New York is terribly overshadowed and/or overlooked by investors. In the best year, 2011, upstate received $106M, but in a low year like 2009, the entire upstate area received only $28M.

---

[6] Note that the NVCA/www.pwcmoneytree.com data does not break out Long Island as a separate region, so in this report, all data for Long Island is aggregated with, and attributed to, New York City.

Who's Investing in New York State? Previously it was determined that New York City VCs deploy about $2B annually, but only 17% (or about $350M) remains in-state. That is about 21% of the total that is received by New York. Where is the rest coming from?

NY $ Comes From	Avg ($M) 2008-2012	Percent
NY	$351	21%
CA	$334	20%
MA	$221	13%
Rest of Country	$368	22%
Undisclosed	$265	16%
Foreign	$114	7%
Total Received	$1,654	100%

Figure 4.2: Where New York Money Comes From

Even though California VCs only send 4% of their monies to New York, it does appear that they are matching the New York City VCs' commitment to New York with about $330M. The rest comes from "all over."

Funding by Industry, New York State. Funding, broken out by industry, is where the real story emerges for New York State. The blue bars in Figure 4.3 indicate overall funding. But notice both green bars. The darker green is for IT, definitely a favored industry in New York State. The lighter green bars are for Creative & Commerce, also definitely favored industries. And actually in 2011 and 2012, Creative & Commerce garnered more investment capital than even IT.

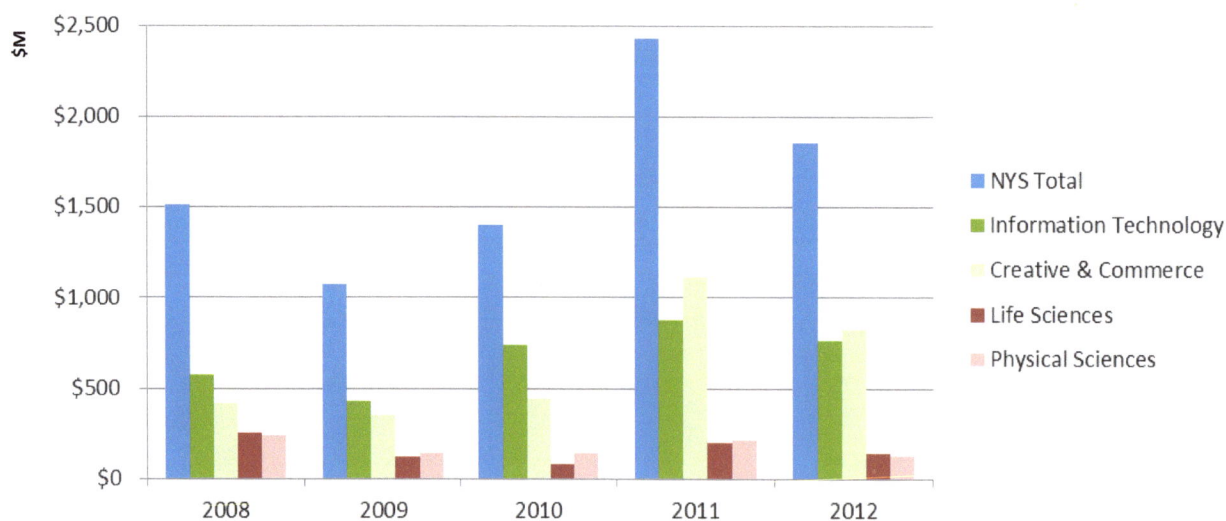

Figure 4.3: VC Investments by Industry, NYS, 2008-2012

In contrast are the red and pink bars: Life Science investing is decreasing, and the small attention it is receiving stands in sharp contrast to IT and Creative & Commerce. The story is the same for the Physical Sciences.

Granular Look. Because this situation is so important to fulfill the hope of successfully commercializing university-based technologies, it is worth taking a granular look at each of these industry segments with exact percentages from 2008 to 2012.

Figure 4.4 shows that IT has long been a favored industry in New York State. If anything, its popularity seems to be increasing in recent years. A major peak in 2010 was observed, when IT consumed 52% of total investments. The average number of deals per year was 126, and the average deal size was $5.4M.

VC $M	2008	2009	2010	2011	2012
NYS Total	$1,513	$1,068	$1,401	$2,429	$1,853
Information Technology	39%	41%	52%	37%	41%
Creative & Commerce	28%	34%	32%	46%	44%
Life Sciences	17%	12%	6%	8%	8%
Physical Sciences	16%	13%	10%	9%	7%

Figure 4.4: VC Investments by Industry, in Percentages

Creative & Commerce have also long been favored industries in New York State. Again, if anything, their popularity seems to be increasing in recent years. A major peak in 2011 was observed, when Creative & Commerce investing exceeded $1B, or 46% of total investments. The average number of deals per year was 105, and the average deal size was $6.0M.

Life Sciences has not been a favored industry in New York State, and its popularity seems to be decreasing in recent years. A new low in 2010 was observed where Life Science investing dropped to $81M, or 6% of total investments. The average number of deals per year was only 21, and the average deal size was $7.4M, actually a bit larger than IT and Creative & Commerce deals.

Physical Sciences has also not been a favored industry in New York State, and its popularity is also decreasing. A new low in 2012 was observed where Physical Science investing dropped to $124M, or only 7% of total investments. The average number of deals per year was 35, and the average deal size was $4.9M, the lowest deal size compared to the other industries.

VC Investing by Industry, 2012. Focusing on 2012, the data in Figure 4.4 can be reconfigured in the form of a pie chart. The visualization of what is happening in New York is dramatic. The overall investing pattern is not consistent with national averages (Figure 4.5) and is unique to New York (Figure 4.6).

IT investing is much more popular in New York than most New Yorkers probably realize. What is really surprising is that Creative & Commerce investing is now exceeding IT. No other venture pie in the world has Creative & Commerce at 44%. Of course, this category includes the legacy industries in New York City, considered one of the most creative cities in the world and the world's capital for commerce. While this investment pattern makes perfect sense, these numbers are not common knowledge even in the New York entrepreneurial community. Certainly no one has yet recognized, in numbers, that the hard sciences are being marginalized in this way. These data may have profound implications for how structures are implemented to grow the innovation economy in New York State.

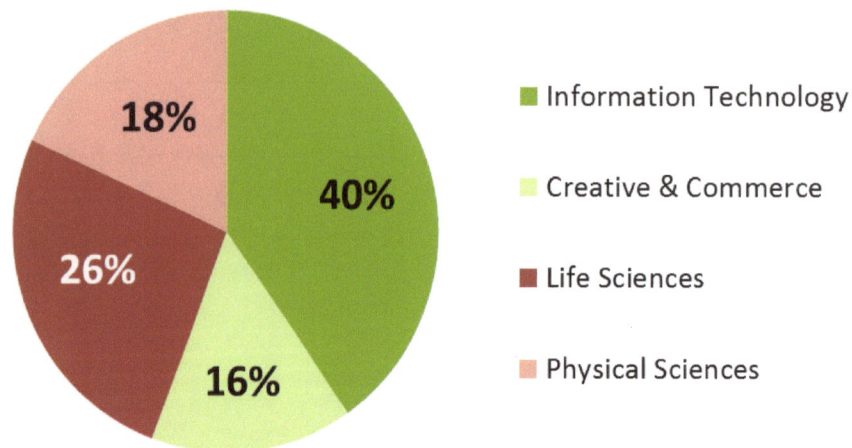

Figure 4.5: VC Investments by Industry, USA, 2012

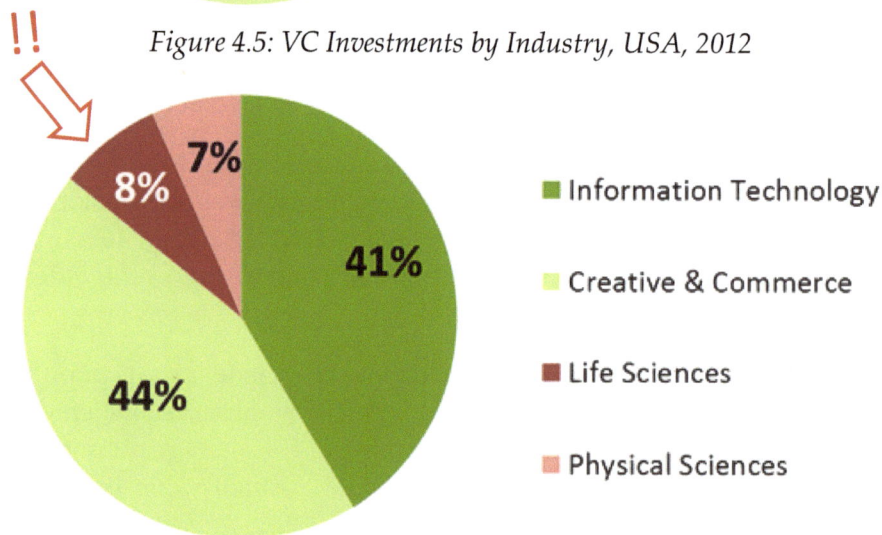

Figure 4.6: VC Investments by Industry, NYS, 2012

Funding by Stage. A look at funding by company development stage is also important. Figure 4.7 shows funding by stage, which is again significantly different for New York than for the rest of the country. Recalling the bar graph for the U.S. shown earlier in Figure 2.8, a trend was observed in that investing was almost 1/3, 1/3, 1/3 for early, expansion, and later stage companies. That is not the pattern here.

In New York State, in 2008, it almost looked like 1/3, 1/3, 1/3, but the trend has moved dramatically to expansion as the favored stage for investors. Seed-stage funding by VCs continues to be at a very low level. This is crucial to note. Internet companies require only small amounts of seed capital to launch. In conjunction with angel monies, a small amount of venture capital might be sufficient to foster the recent success in New York City. But for hard science start-ups, large amounts of cash are needed even at the seed stage and this low level of seed activity is not enough to bring companies through the Valley of Death.

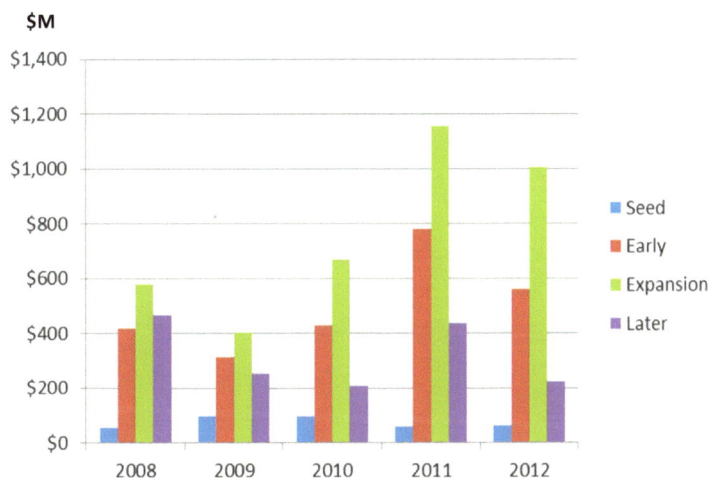

NY Only	Avg	Avg %
Seed	$74	4%
Early	$500	30%
Expansion	$761	46%
Later	$318	19%
Total	$1,653	100%

Figure 4.7: NYS Funding by Stage, 2008-2012

Section Summary. New York State has received, on average, $1.7B annually in VC investments in the last five years. A woefully small amount (3%, or around $50M) has gone to upstate, so clearly the monies are really for New York City. On average, 21% has come from in-state VCs, a similar amount from California, and the rest from elsewhere. Forty-six percent of the investing has been in expansion stage companies. The real story is in the industries receiving capital: an amazing 85% is being committed to the digital technologies and only 15% goes to the hard sciences. Again, the investing excitement over digital technologies is in New York City, while upstate does not even appear to be on the radar for these industry sectors.

All these trends could mean that, every year, the chances of a seed stage life science company in upstate receiving capital from a New York City VC is: *$1.7B (NYS total) x 21% (from NYC) x 8% (to life sciences) x 3% (to Upstate) x 3% (to seed stage) = almost zero.* The chances are even worse for a physical science company, and the odds are also not good for science companies of either type in New York City.

VI. Academic R&D Expenditures

At this point, the reader should have a thorough understanding of venture investing patterns nationally and in New York State. But venture capital supports the translation of academic R&D into viable companies (at least that is the working premise here), and a thorough understanding of academic R&D nationally or in New York State has not yet been provided. This section examines those data.

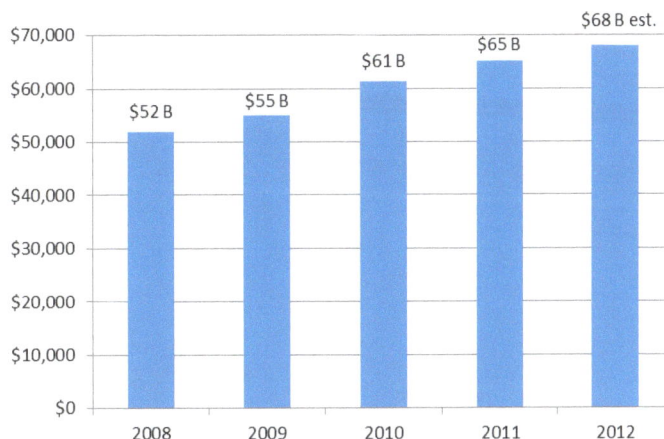

Figure 5.1: National University R&D Expenditures

University R&D, Nationally. Very much in contrast to venture capital investments that are subject to market variability, university-based R&D funding, primarily supplied by the federal government, is subject to federal agency dynamics, political pressures, and the interests of academic scholars. Expenditures rise steadily each year seemingly independent of market conditions. As shown in Figure 5.1, nationally, R&D investing was at about $50B in 2008, and by 2011, it was already at about $65B. This represents a 30% increase in four years.[7]

With this $65B, universities performed more than half of the nation's total academic research. The other half was conducted at federal laboratories, non-university affiliated medical facilities, and other research institutions. Total academic research exceeds well over $100B annually, representing a significant portion of total U.S. R&D.

The federal government provides the bulk of these funds. Six agencies provide almost all federal support—the National Institutes of Health, National Science Foundation, Department of Defense, National Aeronautics and Space Administration, Department of Energy, and Department of Agriculture.

Top States' Five-year Trends. Figure 5.2 shows the university-based R&D expenditures of some of the top states. California has historically held and continues to hold the number

---

[7] While there is a year lag at the NSF in reporting R&D numbers and 2012 data is not yet available, we can probably expect that the national R&D total for 2012 might be around $68B.

one position. New York has historically held and continues to rank number two, followed by Texas, Maryland, Pennsylvania, and Massachusetts, in that order.

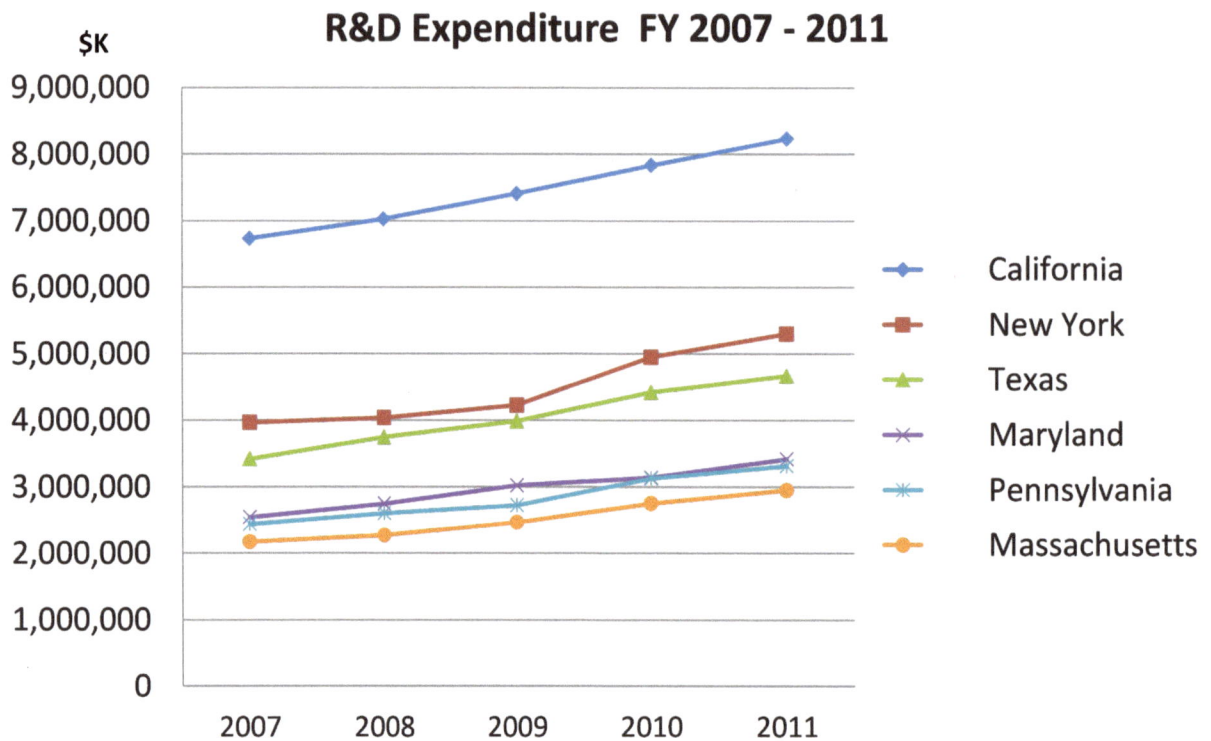

Figure 5.2: R&D Expenditures, by State, Five Year Trends

Top States' 2010 Snapshot. Using 2010 as a representative year, Figure 5.3 shows the specific amounts of R&D expenditures for each of the states along with their percent of the nation's total.

Rank	Division and State	2010 R&D ($M)	Percent
1	California	$7,831	13%
2	New York	$4,951	8%
3	Texas	$4,418	7%
4	Maryland	$3,139	5%
5	Pennsylvania	$3,127	5%
6	Massachusetts	$2,750	4%
	Rest of Country	$35,019	57%
	Total	$61,235	100%

Figure 5.3: R&D Expenditures, by State, 2010

With these data points, another one of Governor Cuomo's Troubling Tech Transfer Facts can now be updated:

- **In 2007**, New York universities ranked second nationally in total research spending with nearly $4B expended annually; California ranked first with $6.5B.

- **In 2011**, New York universities ranked second nationally in total research spending with $5.3B expended annually; California ranked first with $8.2B.

- **In 2012**, expenditures in New York can be estimated to be over $5.5B, and California expenditures at about $8.5B.

States with >$1B in R&D. The national R&D statistics stand in sharp contrast to the venture capital data. Venture capital is highly concentrated in California, Massachusetts, and New York, while the nation's intellectual capital and research expertise is much more broadly distributed. In fact, there are 20 states that expend at or over $1B annually in R&D just at their universities.

For those researchers/entrepreneurs who are not in California, it is unfortunate that over 50% of all venture capital dollars goes to California, when so much "leveragable" intellectual capital and high-level university-based research resides in and is well distributed throughout the entire U.S.

New York State Five-year Trends. Figure 5.4 is a bar graph that shows five-year R&D trends and a steady increase in expenditures in New York State. As already noted, in 2010 R&D levels nearly hit $5B and have now exceeded that.

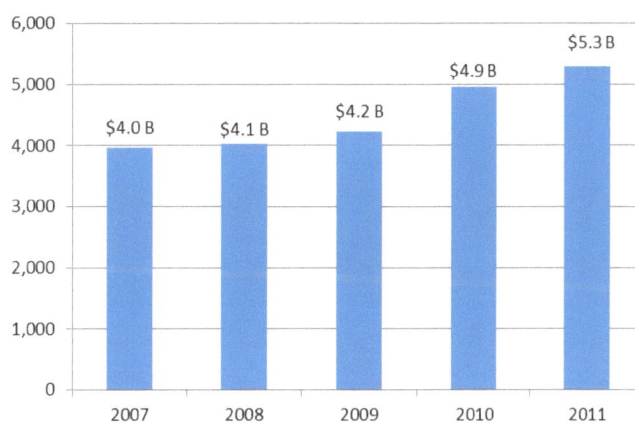

Figure 5.4: R&D Expenditures, NYS

Including Brookhaven National Lab on Long Island, which expends another $650M annually, the New York State total for research funding stands at or over $6B annually. That is a huge investment in basic research. And again, it ticks up year after year.

Upstate-Downstate Split. Given these high expenditures, how are they divided between upstate and downstate? The answer is: very evenly. Figure 5.5 uses 2010 as a representative year, but any year could have been used. The balance every year is nearly 50:50 with downstate always slightly over 50% and upstate slightly under 50% (although adding in Brookhaven tips the balance in downstate's favor). But regardless, at number two in the nation for R&D, this is a very smart state, and its intellectual strength is quite evenly distributed.

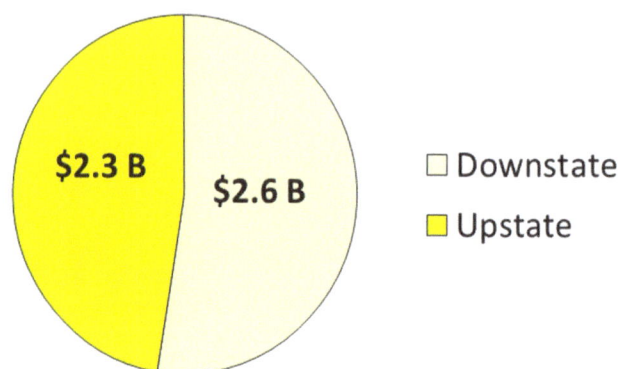

Figure 5.5: NYS R&D Expenditure Split, 2010

Top Research Universities. Figure 5.6 shows New York's top research universities and their specific expenditure levels. Only universities exceeding $70M annually were included on the list. Columbia and Cornell lead the pack with over $800M and $750M, respectively.

Rank	Top Research Universities	2010 R&D Expenditures ($K)
1	Columbia U	$807,235
2	Cornell U	$749,721
3	U of Rochester	$414,655
4	Mt. Sinai School of Medicine	$370,666
5	NYU	$365,944
6	SUNY Albany	$359,364
7	SUNY Buffalo	$349,670
8	Yeshiva U	$314,240
9	Rockefeller U	$265,750
10	SUNY Stony Brook	$204,728
11	Syracuse U	$107,024
12	Rensselaer Polytechnic Institute	$83,952
13	SUNY Binghamton	$72,057
	Total for these 13 Universities	$4,465,006
	% of State Total	*90%*
	15 schools at $10-50M each, totalling ...	$395,086
	51 schools at $100K to $10M each, totaling ...	$90,901
	Total for NYS	**$4,950,993**

Figure 5.6: Top Research Universities in NYS

These thirteen institutions represent 90% of the state's total expenditures. Fifteen other universities share another 8% of the total by expending between $10M and $50M annually in R&D, and 51 smaller schools share in the final 2% with between $100K and $10M in R&D annually each.

Upstate-Downstate Split. Figure 5.7 categorizes the universities as upstate or downstate. Upstate has four major players in Cornell, University of Rochester, the University at Albany, and the University at Buffalo, with Syracuse University, RPI, and Binghamton University still making the top list but with smaller contributions.

Downstate has six major players as listed, with a large gap between them and the smaller schools, all coming in at less than $70M each.

Top Universities, Upstate	2010 R&D Expenditures ($K)
Cornell U	$749,721
U of Rochester	$414,655
SUNY Albany	$359,364
SUNY Buffalo	$349,670
Syracuse U	$107,024
RPI	$83,952
SUNY Binghamton	$72,057
Total for 7 Universities	$2,136,443
% of State Upstate Total	91%
Others at less than $70K	$213,466
Total for Upstate	$2,349,909

Top Universities, Downstate	2010 R&D Expenditures ($K)
Columbia U	$807,235
Mt. Sinai	$370,666
NYU	$365,944
Yeshiva U	$314,240
Rockefeller U	$265,750
SUNY Stony Brook	$204,728
Total for 6 Universities	$2,328,563
% of State Total	90%
Others at less than $70K	$272,521
Total for Downstate	$2,601,084

Figure 5.7: Top Research Universities in NYS, split Upstate, Downstate

Regional Breakdown. For those who view the state as segregated into ten regional councils, Figure 5.8 provides data. Mid-Hudson, North Country, and Mohawk Valley are the only regions that lack the major university powerhouses that the other regions enjoy.

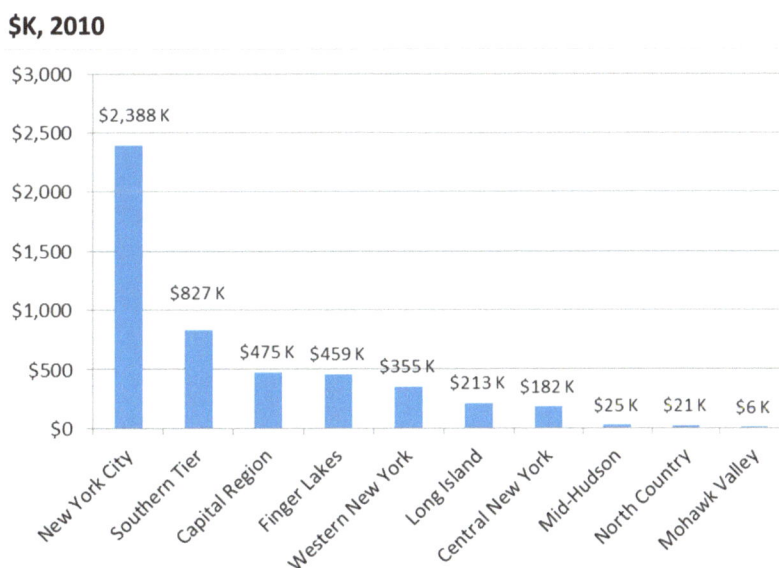

Figure 5.8: University R&D, split by 10 Regional Councils

R&D by Industry/Sector. Unusual patterns for New York State start to emerge when looking at the breakdown of R&D by industry/sector.

33

Nationally, over the last twenty years, the distribution of academic R&D expenditures across the broad scientific fields has shifted in favor of Life Sciences and away from Physical Sciences. As shown in Figure 5.9, the Life Sciences now represent the largest share (well over 50%) of expenditures in academic R&D. However, in New York State, Life Sciences represent 65% of the total. The New York State pie is skewed because of downstate New York, where academic research is fully three-quarters in Life Science fields.

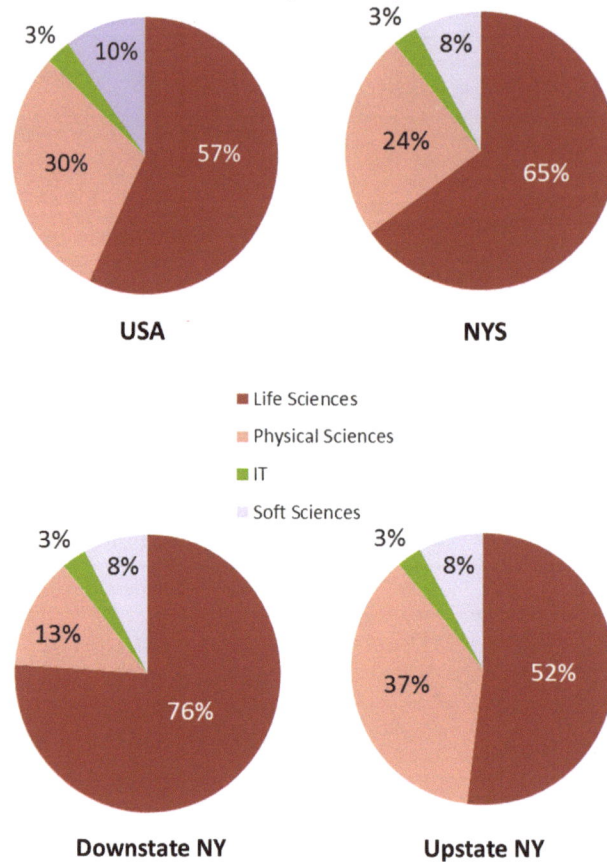

Figure 5.9: University R&D, by Industry/Sector

Specifically, downstate Life Science research is at 76% of the downstate total. This is the strongest imbalance toward Life Sciences in the nation. New York City's Life Science cluster includes nine major academic institutions. In addition, there are 26 additional research facilities and medical centers and 58 hospitals. NYC was the second largest recipient of NIH funding from 1999 through 2008. Relative to Life Science research, upstate is more typical at 52%, as is California at 59%. Massachusetts' university R&D is well balanced at 44% for Life and 43% for Physical Sciences.

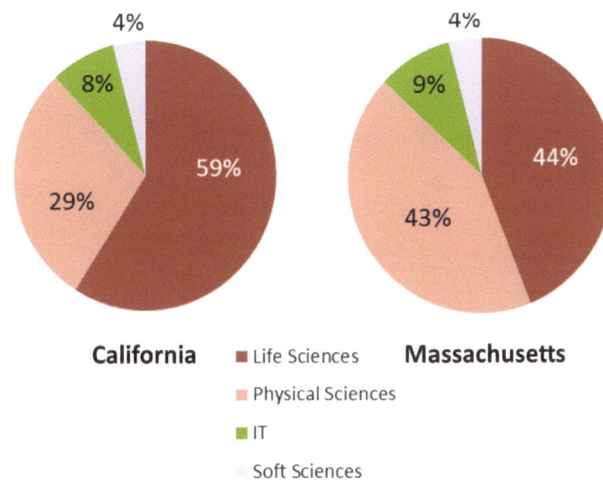

Figure 5.10: University R&D, by Industry/Sector

Section Summary. While venture capital is subject to market pressures, university-based R&D is subject to political factors and the interests of researchers and increases annually at a fairly steady rate. Levels are now topping $65B annually for the nation and over $100B, if federal labs are included.

New York State ranks number two in the nation, second only to California, expending well over $5B annually at its universities (nearly twice that of Massachusetts) and about $6B when Brookhaven is included. It also hosts other prestigious research institutions such as Roswell Park and Sloan Kettering Cancer Institutes, which further increase total academic R&D spending.

R&D expenditures are divided almost evenly between upstate and downstate, with Life Sciences as a dominant industry/sector, particularly downstate.

What's Next? A working premise here is that venture capital is required to translate academic R&D into viable companies.

- A thorough understanding of venture investing patterns has been provided.

- It has been shown that academic R&D is well funded both in the U.S. and in New York State.

- If the reader correctly understands the data already provided, suspicions may be rising that the interests of VCs and academic researchers are increasingly misaligned.

To validate (or refute) these growing suspicions, the VC and R&D data were directly juxtaposed.

VII. Mismatched Interests

U.S. R&D vs. VC, juxtaposed. In this section, the VC and R&D data is directly juxtaposed to determine how well the interests of the VCs and the academic researchers correlate. Using 2010 as a representative year, the R&D and VC numbers are broken down by industry sector. As below, the *mismatch* between R&D spending and VC investing in the U.S. is illustrated with the data placed side-by-side. Note especially the life science bars.

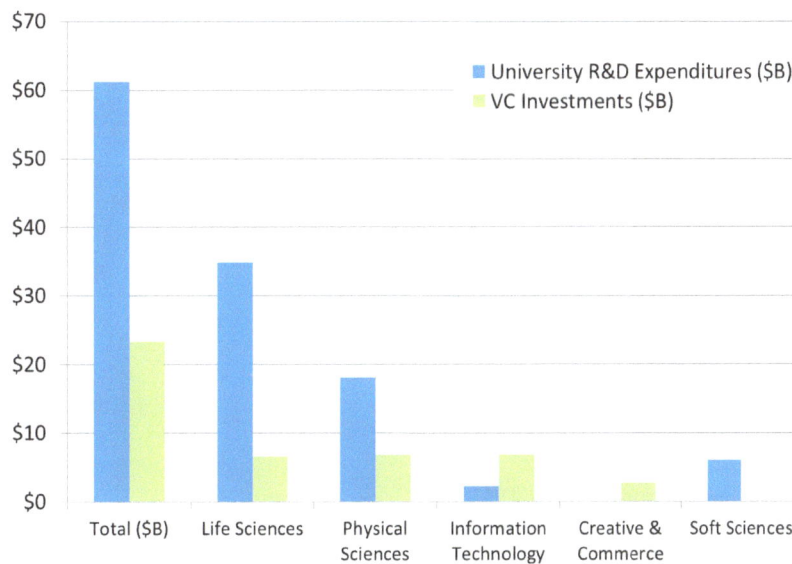

Figure 6.1: US R&D vs VC, 2010

New York State R&D vs. VC, juxtaposed. The mismatch appears to be particularly dramatic in New York State. As shown below, in 2010, New York expended $5B annually for university-based hard science research, with ~65% invested in Life Science. Meanwhile, venture capital investing in New York is largely ignoring the hard sciences, especially the Life Sciences, and favoring Information Technology.

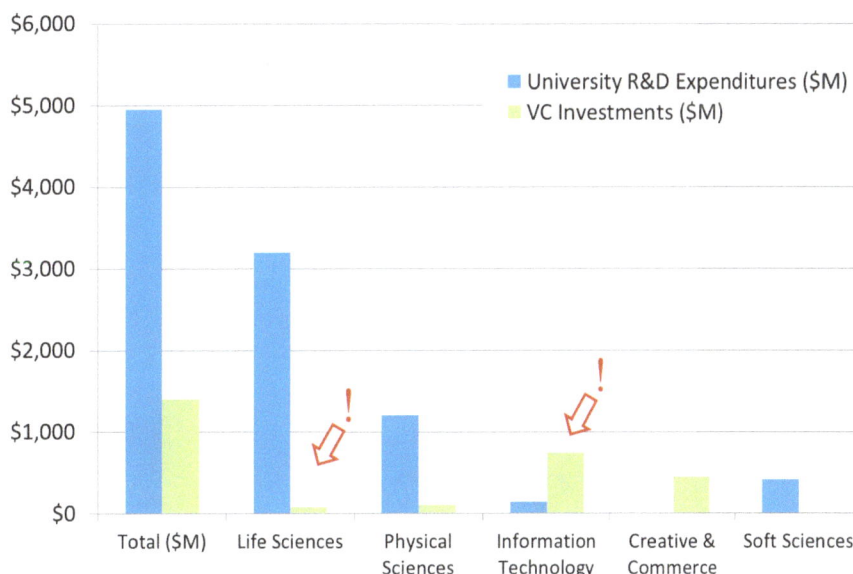

Figure 6.2: NYS R&D vs VC, 2010

Upstate New York R&D vs. VC. Again, with 2010 as a representative year, the well-known and discouraging story for upstate New York is that VC is literally invisible—i.e., it's not there. However, the university R&D expenditures are strong, among the highest in the nation. The economic developers in the region are pinning their hopes on biotech as the future of the Upstate economy. It is difficult to know how that is going to happen with almost no venture interest.

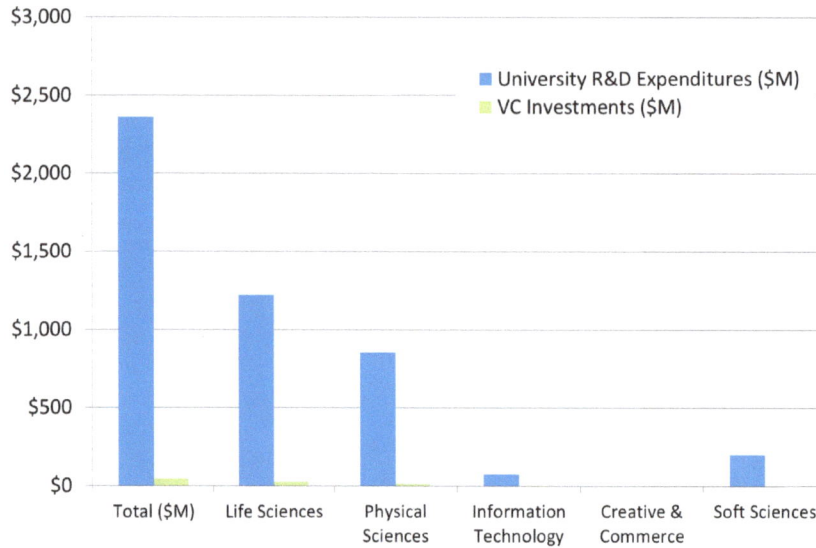

Figure 6.3: Upstate NY R&D vs VC, 2010

Downstate New York R&D vs. VC. 2010 is still the year, but now the focus is on downstate New York, where VCs don't look interested in the Life Sciences either. In fact, we could probably state that the *Life Sciences are being ignored* and the favored industries are again IT (by far) and Creative & Commerce.

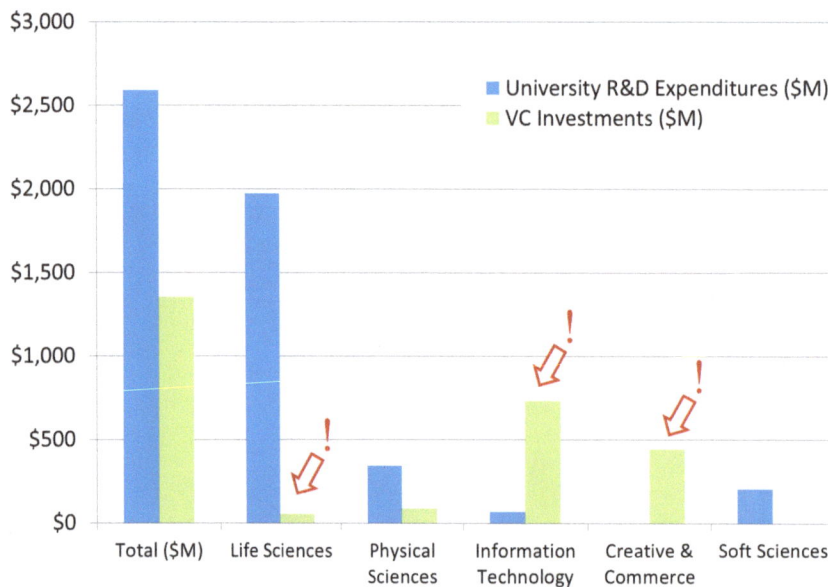

Figure 6.4: Downstate NY R&D vs VC, 2010

Massachusetts R&D vs. VC. A comparison can be made between downstate New York (basically New York City) to Massachusetts (basically Boston). The bars in Figure 6.5 indicate a different world in Boston. The reader might consider the question: *Would a life science company prefer to launch in Boston or NYC? Or actually, what would the preference be for any kind of university start-up besides IT?*

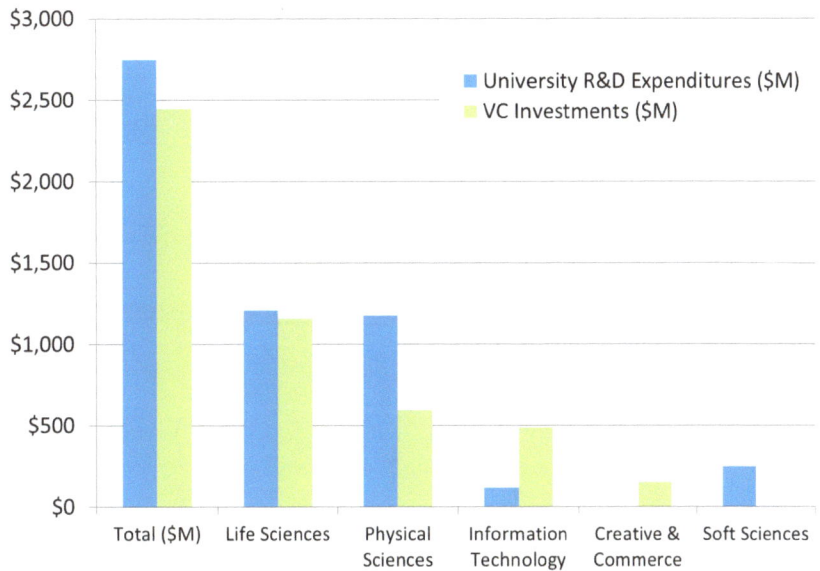

Figure 6.5: Massachusetts R&D vs VC, 2010

California R&D vs. VC. When launching a science start-up, the odds of receiving capital are much more favorable in California than in New York. IT is very popular for investors in California, but the Physical Sciences attract significant venture investment as well. Life Sciences are down a bit.

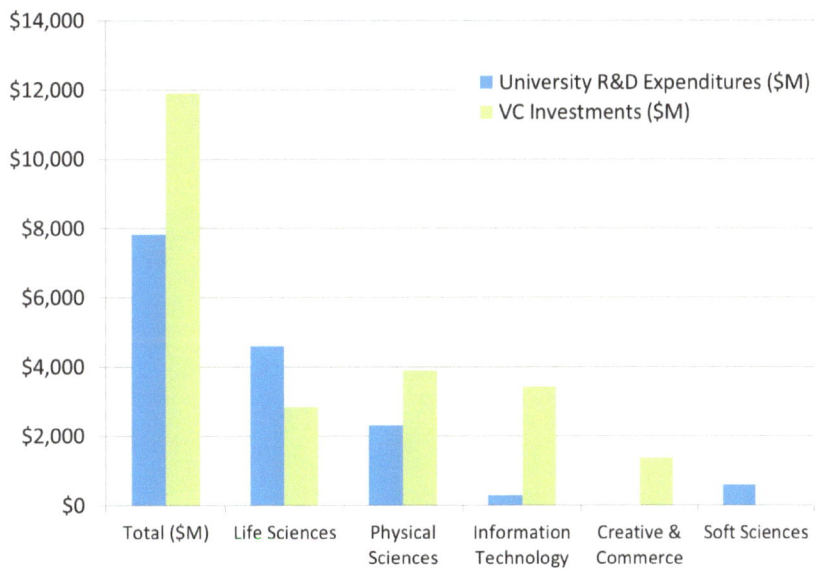

Figure 6.6: California R&D vs VC, 2010

It's Getting Worse. This report is raising concerns about venture investing patterns relative to the Life Sciences. An article appeared recently, reporting that the situation relative to life science investing may be getting worse.[8]

Life sciences VC funding took double-digit dip in 2012

February 12, 2013 – 11:03 am by Chris

By Mia Burns

U.S. venture capital funding within the life sciences sector slid 14 percent in dollars and 7 percent in deals last year, according to a new PwC report titled *Double-digit dip.* The report included data from the MoneyTree Report from PricewaterhouseCoopers LLP and the National Venture Capital Association based on data provided by Thomson Reuters. Venture capitalists invested a total of $6.6 billion in 779 life sciences deals during the year, compared to $7.7 billion in 836 deals during 2011. The number of life sciences companies receiving venture capital funding reached the lowest level since 1995, which was unprecedented. Only 135 companies received funding in 2012.

Upstate Perceptions. Given the data shown in Figure 6.3, it is ironic that there is a perception in upstate New York that the region's future economic strength lies in the Life Sciences. The following excerpt is taken from a Zogby Survey of upstate New York employers and shows that "life sciences and high technology are seen as having the highest potential for job creation" in the region.[9]

Zogby Analytics Summary

While business officials have deep concerns about the future of upstate, they have invested and promise to invest more in their businesses.

Current economic conditions and economic development assistance received low marks, but there is an appetite for growth and adding jobs.

Taxes and health care costs are the top concerns of business officials, followed by the overall upstate economy and workforce availability.

A majority claims New York has poor opportunity for young people, business startups, and welcoming new employers, **but** many see the state as good or improving.

Life sciences and high technology are seen as having the highest potential for job creation.

---

[8] www.pharmalive.com/life-sciences-vc-funding-took-double-digit-dip-2012

[9] Zogby Survey of Upstate NY Employers, John Zogby of Zogby International, March 2013, commissioned by The Buffalo Niagara Partnership.

40

The results from the Zogby poll shown indicate that among all the industries listed, the highest percentage of all respondents stated that the Life Sciences would have the highest rate of growth for job creation **and private sector investments** in upstate NY.[10]

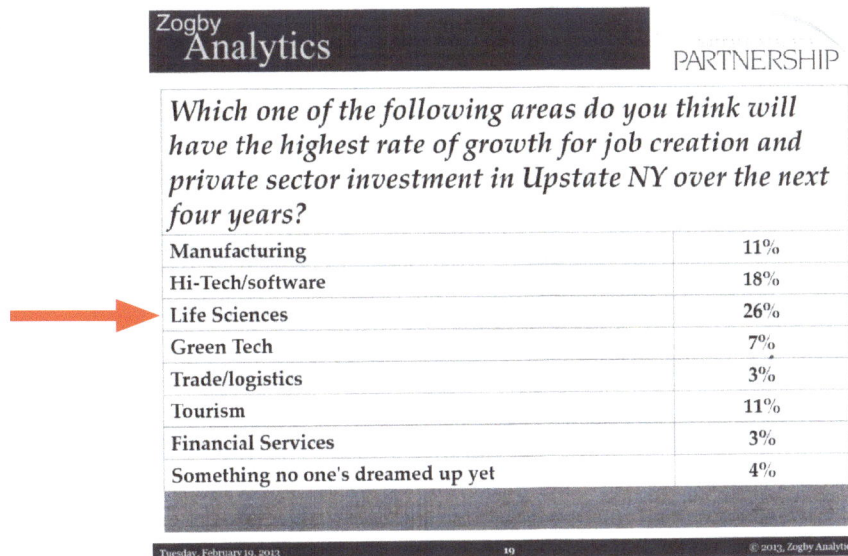

Zogby
Analytics   PARTNERSHIP

Which one of the following areas do you think will have the highest rate of growth for job creation and private sector investment in Upstate NY over the next four years?

Manufacturing	11%
Hi-Tech/software	18%
Life Sciences	26%
Green Tech	7%
Trade/logistics	3%
Tourism	11%
Financial Services	3%
Something no one's dreamed up yet	4%

Tuesday, February 19, 2013   19   © 2013, Zogby Analytics

Not to burst anyone's bubble, but it is difficult to know how that is going to happen with the current patterns in VC investing as they are and as observed in this report.

Section Summary. There is a very positive perception that the future economic strength of New York State (at least upstate) depends on developing the Life Sciences and that somehow the region will attract private sector investments. This could be a logical thought since, as in California and Massachusetts, the majority of New York's university R&D is focused on Life Sciences. But in New York, venture capital is almost exclusively focused on digital technologies while the hard (both Life and Physical) sciences are being ignored. This mismatch, or disconnect, must be given serious consideration if our plans for economic success are to be realized.

---

[10] Zogby Survey of Upstate NY Employers, John Zogby of Zogby International, March 2013, commissioned by The Buffalo Niagara Partnership.

VIII. Observations and Comments

The very good news of this study is that while maintaining a strong position as second in the nation in terms of university-based R&D expenditures, New York State has greatly improved its position as a recipient of investment funds to support entrepreneurship. This phenomenon is entirely led by New York City, whose innovation ecosystem has undergone astonishing growth over the past five years. The challenge within this good news is that the growth in New York City has been almost exclusively in the Internet sector, not in the commercialization of R&D. The challenge for the rest of the state, and upstate in particular, is that they have participated hardly at all in this growth.

Thus, active pursuit of an innovation agenda for New York State is smart and timely. Yet, there are nuances within the entrepreneurial ecosystem that if not addressed and accommodated could potentially short-circuit these efforts. More than a nuance, as reported in this paper, is a lack of alignment between venture capital and academic R&D in New York State, in both type and quantity. Understanding this misalignment is key to driving policy that will be both responsive and effective.

One outcome of this misalignment is the scarcity of thriving innovation-based entrepreneurial firms, especially in upstate New York. Given New York's large pool of intellectual property created through university research, it is easy to imagine that better "technology harvesting" will increase the economic yield. It is a real challenge, though, for such companies to grow without available investment capital to provide both financial support and the many intangibles that venture capitalists provide to help nascent companies grow.

Growing a successful innovation ecosystem in upstate New York is not just a matter of better technology transfer. With so much of the intellectual property in the Life and Physical sciences, a formula for profitable companies will require significant time and adequate investment capital. As this report shows, investment capital is hardly available at all for this task. Life science investment requires a great deal of domain knowledge, in addition to the particular patience required due to the regulatory steps required. While public funds perform an important function priming the pump, new investors must also be identified and attracted to become engaged in New York State.

It must be understood that not all "tech" is the same. This report offers a distinction between "soft" and "hard" tech that may be useful. Hard tech is <u>literally</u> harder to advance given the greater complexity and challenges of developing science into technology, refining technology into products, and testing those products while maintaining a clear sense of the market. Such opportunities require investors who are not only patient, but also have some knowledge of the more complex domains involved. Very different is "soft tech," which generally relies on digital or Internet-based technology that is well understood, and whose major challenges have to do with application, market savvy, and execution. These latter areas are less expensive to fund, and are generally easier for an intelligent non-expert to understand.

New York City is capitalizing on its strengths in soft tech. Its huge customer base, global reach, and most importantly, its domain expertise in fields as diverse as finance and fashion, make it a likely leader in this space. This is very timely for the New York City economy, its entrepreneurial community, including its investors. As a result, hard-tech entrepreneurship both downstate and upstate has been marginalized. This is consistent with what appears to be a growing mismatch between the interests of university researchers and VCs nationally, but the misalignment is particularly dramatic in New York.

New York City will hopefully sustain its entrepreneurial momentum as its entrepreneurs continue to create innovative digital capabilities around its legacy industries in creative (media, entertainment, advertising, fashion, education) and commerce (finance, business, retail, distribution). However, upstate's strengths, clusters, university R&D, and legacy industries are all in hard sciences. Legacy industries include optics, photonics, electronics, instrumentation, biotech, medical devices, computer hardware, etc. At this point, its entrepreneurial ecosystems are "invisible" to VCs and struggling.

In conclusion, this report offers a challenge, an opportunity, and a consideration of actions for the road ahead.

The Challenge. Improving the performance of the New York State innovation ecosystem, especially upstate, to successfully commercialize its technology into vibrant, meaningful firms will require stronger, and perhaps new, ecosystems of investors and others to create and grow businesses built on Life and Physical Sciences. The current gap between investors and academic researchers may require creative actions, for instance, engaging investor communities in Massachusetts, California, and elsewhere.

The Opportunity. The success of the New York City paradigm in growing many entrepreneurial businesses over the past five years, *without significant contribution from university R&D,* must be explored for its potential economic benefit upstate. START-UP NY offers the opportunity for many kinds of university-business alliances to form, other than those based on the hard sciences. Engaging New York City business leaders in designing mutually beneficial partnerships to grow opportunities upstate based on this model seems an obvious step to explore.

The Road Ahead. The Entrepreneurship in New York project is committed to supporting a vibrant entrepreneurial ecosystem and a strong innovation economy across New York State. It is designed to tackle multiple goals and disseminate analytical findings by issuing a series of reports.

The next report will provide a baseline assessment of university-based entrepreneurship using specific metrics, including number of university spin-outs, sector performance, regional performance, and economic impacts. Future reports will measure the success of current initiatives to stimulate the translation of innovation into commerce. These reports are intended to serve as a baseline against which progress of New York's innovation agenda can be measured.

Collectively, the ENY project reports will deepen the knowledge base of regional stakeholders so they can respond creatively and actively to the challenges and opportunities in the global economy and spur innovation and entrepreneurship in New York State.

Appendix A: Summary of Misalignments

The Misalignments between Venture Capital and University-Based R&D: A National Look

Variable	University-based R&D	Venture capital
Market Pressure vs Political Pressure	Expenditures, mostly from the federal government, are now topping $65B annually for the nation and are over $100B if spending at federal labs is included.	Subject to market pressures and can be variable; VC's are currently investing about $30B annually on start-ups.
Spending on Hard Sciences	The federal government continues to increase spending almost exclusively in the hard sciences.	In recent years, VC investing in the hard sciences has declined steadily.
Geographic Distribution	Conducted to a significant extent in every state in the country. There are 20 states that expend at or over $1B annually, and even more states join the list if spending at federal labs is included. But the majority of these states are in VC "fly over zones".	Highly concentrated in three states, California, Massachusetts, and New York; most states have little access to VC and receive between 0-1% of the nation's total.
Preferred Industries	The conversation about accelerating the commercialization of university-based research is happening in nearly every state in the US because nearly every state has major universities and/or federal research facilities and has an interest in capitalizing on its hard science research and creating an innovation economy.	A stong historical focus on IT, software, and the internet. Within the last five years, the trend has intensified and the majority of VC investments are now being made in IT and Creative & Commerce (as these later industries become digital and mobile).
Needs	30 million people die annually from disease; the US continues to seek energy independence; the military must continuously upgrade and advance its weapons systems. Federal and state governments understand these NEEDS and are committed to supporting the research in the hard sciences at universities across the country where technologies to solve these problems are being developed.	VCs NEED to get a return on their investment (ROI). If they are getting returns with companies in software/IT/internet, then that is what they need to focus on. If the market is demanding these products and services, then that is where the VCs will place their bets.
Translational Efficiency	According to the Global Innovation Index 2012, the USA is #10 worldwide for R&D	According to the Global Innovation Index 2012, the US ranks #70 for "translational efficiency".

The Misalignments between Venture Capital and University-Based R&D: A Focus on New York State

Variables	*University-based R&D*	*Venture capital*
NYS Leads in Academic R&D but Lags in Venture Capital.	NYS is #2 in the nation. There are 13 major research universities, expending from $70M to $800M annually in R&D, totaling well over $5B. Adding in Brookhaven National Labs, brings the total to about $6B annually!	Relative to California and Massachusetts, NYS doesn't receive that much, doesn't have that much under management, and doesn't keep as much in-state. NYS has about 6% of the national total, meaning that on average NYS receives about $1.7B per year.
Geographic Distributions.	Well balanced between Upstate and Downstate; Upstate invests about $2.3B annually (nearly the same as the state of North Carolina) and Downstate invests about $2.6B annually	Downstate, particularly NYC, receives 97% of the venture capital in the state while the entire Upstate region receives 3%. Upstate NY is a venture capital desert.
Hard Sciences Downstate	Of the $2.6B in Downstate R&D, 76% of all R&D Downstate is in the Life Sciences and 13% is in the Physical Sciences	Of the nearly $2B in venture capital in NYC, 8% goes to the Life Sciences, and 7% goes to the Physical Sciences.
Hard Sciences Upstate	Of the $2.3B in Upstate R&D, 52% of all R&D Upstate is in the Life Science and 32% is in the Physical Sciences	There is extremely little VC investing Upstate in either the Life or Physical Science, e.g., $.042B total in 2010
Digital Technologies Downstate	Only 4% of Downstate university R&D expenditures are in IT, and essentially none in Creative and Commerce	In recent years, NYC has become a "digital media mecca". NYS/NYC now exceeds Massachusetts/Boston is investing in the internet and other digital technologies. In 2012, 41% of the venture capital was committed to IT opportunities and 44% went to Creative & Commerce.
Digital Technologies Upstate	As at Downstate universities, only 4% of Upstate R&D expenditures are in IT, and essentially none in Creative and Commerce	Upstate entrepreneurs are really not involved in the Creative & Commerce industries and almost no investments are being made Upstate in IT, e.g., $.003B in 2010.
NY Investment patterns are unlike anywhere in the world.	University R&D expenditures are not being matched to VC investments in NY.	California and Massachusetts R&D expenditures are better matched to their VC expenditures. More goes to the hard sciences and much less goes to Creative & Commerce.

Appendix B: Methodology

Multiple Methodologies. As its name implies, the Entrepreneurship in New York project is intended to study many aspects of entrepreneurship in the state of New York, particularly university-based entrepreneurship, through the application of several methodologies, including:

1. Defining, collecting, and analyzing relevant metrics from primary data sources, such as university technology transfer offices and university-based spin-outs;

2. Reviewing and summarizing key findings from predecessor reports that also address aspects related to New York State entrepreneurship;

3. Carefully sorting, analyzing, and benchmarking data from highly regarded and reliable publically available sources on matters such as venture capital investments and academic R&D expenditures; and

4. Conducting interviews and focus groups with representatives from myriad stakeholder organizations regarding their views on the interpretation of the data, personal perspectives on the subject, and anecdotal experiences.

All of these methodologies will be brought to bear while progressing through the ENY project and issuing reports. This report, however, was primarily focused on the third methodology cited above. The focus was on collecting and analyzing hard data from publically available sources to provide an **objective assessment** on the status of venture capital investments and R&D expenditures in New York State. Publically available data on national matters of interest is particularly useful in benchmarking New York against California and Massachusetts. There is assurance that we are reliably comparing "apples to apples" and that selected metrics are not being interpreted differently from state to state. Also the use of hard data is unrelated to anyone's opinion but is merely a presentation of numbers. While implications can be discussed, the numbers being provided by publically available sources do not carry with them an associated bias.

Venture Capital Data. All venture capital data in this report was derived from the publically accessible searchable database at www.pwcmoneytree.com, as well as the National Venture Capital Association (NVCA) Yearbooks from 2008 through 2013, which are all downloadable online.

The NVCA collects and analyzes venture capital fundraising, investing, and exit statistics in conjunction with its research partners PricewaterhouseCoopers and Thomson Reuters. NVCA/PWC/Reuters is regarded by the venture capital community as one of the most, if not the most, comprehensive and accurate source for all venture capital and private equity investment information.

Through many hours of tedious labor, the data in this report was sorted from the PWC online data base by state, by industry, by stage, and by year and then reconfigured in many different ways into all the data tables appearing in Sections III, IV, and V. The annual NVCA reports were particularly helpful, and served as the primary source, for assembling information related to internet-investing. Other than calculating an average there was no need to apply any complicated mathematical or statistical analysis methods.

Academic R&D Data. All data pertaining to academic R&D in this report was derived from the National Science Foundation (NSF) Higher Education Research and Development (HERD) Reports from 2008 through 2011, which, like the NVCA reports, can all be downloaded online. The HERD Survey collects information annually from nearly a thousand research-performing academic institutions on R&D expenditures by academic field, as well as by source of fund and is the primary data source for these expenditures in the U.S. and outlying areas.

As with the VC data, the R&D data presented here was sorted from the downloaded databases by state, by region, by industry/sector, and by year and then reconfigured in many different ways into all the data tables appearing in Section V.

Matching VC and R&D Data. The intent in this report was to "match up" venture capital investment with R&D investment to determine if there was alignment or misalignment between the interests of VCs and university-based researchers. To do that, it was necessary to create a common language between the data sources being used prior to commencement of this project.

The NVCA uses 16 categories to define the investments and deals in the VC community. The NSF uses 36 categories to define areas of fundable research being conducted at universities. These categorizations were too granular for purposes of the ENY study. For this reason, the first step was to create a terminology alignment table that would regroup and reduce the NVCA and NSF categories into broad categories. As was apparent throughout this document, the focus was on looking at four of five primary industry sectors:

- Life Sciences

- Physical Sciences

- Information Technology

- Creative & Commerce

The way in which the NVCA and NSF categories were grouped for purposes of this study is shown in Figure B-1.

Both the NVCA and the NSF track funding for the Life Sciences, the Physical Sciences, and Information Technology. But it is really only the NVCA that tracks investments in the Creative & Commerce industries. And it is really only within universities that the social sciences are supported with research expenditures as tracked by the NSF.

Other References. Finally, a few other report references where integrated for commentary as needed, including:

- Zogby Survey of Upstate New York Employers, John Zogby of Zogby International, March 2013, commissioned by The Buffalo Niagara Partnership;

- Global Innovation Index 2012. Ref: www.economist.com /node/21531002; and

- A brief reference regarding VC investing in the life sciences taken from www.pharmalive.com/life-sciences-vc-funding-took-double-digit-dip-2012.

There are many other excellent reports that provide significant insights into the status of entrepreneurship in New York, and several of these will be referenced in a subsequent report.

ENY Classification	NVCA/PWC/Reuters Classification for VC Investments	NSF Classification for Academic R&D
LIFE SCIENCES	Biotechnology Medical Devices and Equipment Healthcare Services	Agricultural sciences Biological sciences Medical sciences Life sciences, nec
PHYSICAL SCIENCES	Industrial/Energy Semiconductors Telecommunications Electronics/Instrumentation Networking and Equipment Computers and Peripherals	Astronomy Chemistry Physics Physical sciences, nec Atmospheric sciences Earth sciences Oceanography Environmental sciences, nec Aeronautical/astronautical engineering Bioengineering/biomedical engineering Chemical engineering Civil engineering Electrical engineering Mechanical engineering Metallurgical/materials engineering Engineering, nec Sciences, nec Mathematical sciences
INFORMATION TECHNOLOGY	Software IT Services	Computer sciences
CREATIVE & COMMERCE	Business Products and Services Consumer Products and Services Media and Entertainment Retailing/Distribution Financial Services	
SOCIAL SCIENCES		Economics Political sciences Sociology Social sciences, nec Psychology Business and management Communications, journalism, and library science Education Humanities Law Social work Visual and performing arts Non-science and engineering, nec

Figure B-1: Terminology Alignment